GODIGITAL
KEEP THE PAST ALIVE!

GODIGITAL
KEEP THE PAST ALIVE!

COLIN BARRETT • STEVE LUCK
ALLEN ZUK • KEITH MARTIN

EVERGREEN

Contents

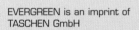

EVERGREEN is an imprint of
TASCHEN GmbH

© 2006 TASCHEN GmbH
Hohenzollernring 53, D-50672 Köln
www.taschen.com

© 2006 The Ilex Press Limited

Publisher: Alastair Campbell
Creative Director: Peter Bridgewater
Editorial Director: Tom Mugridge
Project Editor: Ben Renow-Clarke
Art Director: Julie Weir
Designer: Ginny Zeal
Design Assistant: Kate Haynes

ISBN-13: 978-3-8228-5791-5
ISBN-10: 3-8228-5791-2

Printed and bound in China

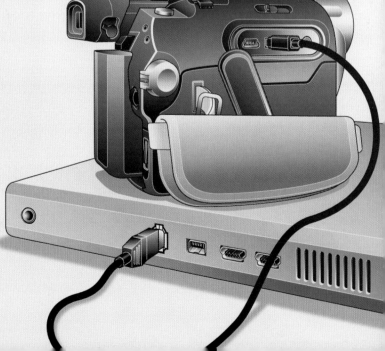

Introduction

There's never been a better time to move into the realm of digital technology. The digital camera is easily outselling its traditional film counterpart. Digital video camcorders make it easy to import your home movies onto your computer, edit them, and burn them to DVD. Music has been ripped kicking and screaming into the digital age thanks to MP3 technology and the ubiquitous iPod. Even phone calls can now be made cheaply and simply via the internet.

So what's so good about digital technology? In a word: Quality. In a few more words: The ability to make perfect copies. There are no gray areas in digital data. If you rip a CD to your computer, you will obtain a perfect copy of that CD. If you copy a photograph from a camera to your computer, you will have a perfect copy of the image; and what's more, you can carry on making perfect copies—the quality of digital data never degrades. Of course, the other great thing about digital data is that once you've transferred it onto your computer, you can do what you like with it. Digital information is easily editable, and you can make changes to copies without harming the original. There's no longer a need for dark rooms full of chemicals or piles of film on the cutting-room floor. With a modern home computer and the right software, you can edit movies, pictures, and music to your heart's content.

Old, damaged photographs can be restored to their former glory quickly and easily. All you need is a scanner, a computer, and a low-cost image-editing package such as Adobe Photoshop Elements (see pages 16–21 for more information on fixing damaged photos).

Okay, we're all agreed on the fact that digital technology's great, but what about all those years of memories that you have stored away in old boxes in the loft—all those vinyl LPs, spools of 8mm film, black-and-white photos, and yellowing documents? That's where *Go Digital* comes in. This book contains all you need to know about converting your old photos, music, and movies into modern digital files.

In the Photography section you'll learn how to scan in your old photographs, restore them by removing any dirt or scratches, and show them to your family or friends via e-mail or the Web.

In the Video section you'll find out how to transfer your dusty VHS tapes or 8mm home movies onto your computer, re-edit them and apply titles and soundtracks, and burn them to DVD, where they can be watched over and over again without fear of damaging them.

In the Music section you'll discover how to transfer your old vinyl records into MP3 files that you can listen to on your digital music player. You'll also get the low-down on digital music, and how to legally purchase and manage it.

In the Documents section you'll see how easy it is to scan your important documents and convert them to editable digital files using OCR, along with storing and organizing information in databases.

In the final section, Communication, you'll learn about technologies such as Skype and weblogging that are keeping people in touch throughout the world.

As you can see, there really has never been a better time to go digital!

Although you can pay to have film transferred professionally to DVD, it's also possible to simply record a projected film using a digital camcorder. The movie can then be copied across to your home computer in one simple step (see pages 44–45 for more information on converting old film).

section one
photographs

photoediting software

Digital photography is now big business; with so many people owning a digital camera, and many more already using or considering buying a computer less as a workstation but more as an entertainment center, it is not surprising that there is an increasing number of photoediting applications available. In fact, typing "free photoediting software" into your computer's Internet search engine will bring up a long list of software that you can download for free.

Free software is useful if all you want to do is very basic editing, but it is unlikely to be able to help you fix damaged or faded prints or transparencies—for that you'll need much more sophisticated examples, which can cost half as much as some digital cameras.

The good news, however, is that with so much competition around, the software developers are anxious for you to try their products. Most of the editing applications available (and all of those used in this section of the book) can be downloaded over the Internet as free trial versions—this way you can try them for yourself and decide which one you think is most appropriate for your needs. A list of Internet addresses can be found on page 152.

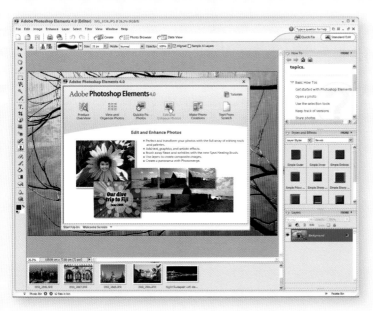

Above Adobe
Photoshop Elements
is one of the most
popular and powerful
low-cost photoediting
applications available.

Popular Software
Below is a brief run down of some of the more popular image-editing software packages available. The list is by no means exhaustive and the accompanying information is intended to act as a review, rather than a guide.

Adobe® Photoshop® Elements
Once thought of as the "cut-down" version of Adobe's professional editing application Photoshop, Elements has been developed over the last couple of years with the digital photographer specifically in mind. It features all the powerful tools and filters necessary to make complex corrections to images, and is ideal for the projects in this section. Elements features an excellent *Help* menu that will take you through the more common image-editing tasks, and the latest version features a powerful *Organizer* tool that will help you to store, sort, and access your images.

Corel® Paint Shop Pro®
Another extremely powerful editing application is Paint Shop Pro. Only available for the Windows platform (that is, it can't be used if you have a Mac),

Paint Shop Pro has near-professional image-editing capabilities, that can be quite difficult to master. The program's other features include a self-contained animation package, called Animation Shop that may or may not appeal to you. Another of Paint Shop Pro's strengths is its Web facilities, which may be valuable if you're intending to set up your own website on which to show some of your work.

FotoFinish Studio

One of the easiest programs to get to grips with, FotoFinish Studio has a very user-friendly interface, allowing you to perform a variety of tasks with ease. Its ease of use, however, is reflected in its fairly limited editing capabilities—but this may well be all you're after. The program's limited editing functions are offset by the excellent sharing features—e-mailing images to family and friends is simply a matter of a couple of clicks. Furthermore, FotoFinish will allow you to set up your own photo gallery on their website free of charge.

Ulead® PhotoImpact®

Offering excellent value for money, PhotoImpact contains very powerful editing capabilities rivalled only by more expensive software. The tools require a fair amount of patience and dedication to learn, but if persevered with, this application can make complex enhancements to your images. Another strength of this particular program is its sharing capabilities. It can automatically "optimize" your images for the Web, create slide shows and Web galleries, and is automatically linked to an online photo company that will host your Web gallery.

Other software

Other popular software for which trial versions are available includes:
• Digital Image Suite
• PhotoStudio
• PhotoPlus
• PhotoSuite
• PhotoLightning

Above There are a great many beginner-level photoediting packages available, such as those shown above. From left to right, they are Paint Shop Pro, PhotoImpact, and FotoFinish Studio.

scanning photographs

Most of us have boxes of family memorabilia that we'd like to preserve—and much of that memorabilia is made up of faded and torn black-and-white or color photographs. But how can we show future generations those who preceded them without damaging these already fragile artifacts? The answer is to create digital versions using an inexpensive desktop scanner. Scanning old photographs is a simple task that only takes a matter of minutes.

Modern scanners are relatively slim and small, and should sit comfortably on the desk, next to your computer. If you've purchased your scanner recently you'll find that it will connect to the computer using either a USB or FireWire cable (see illustration to the right). Along with the scanner will be a disc that contains the scanner's control software. If you haven't used your scanner before, simply insert the disc and follow the installation instructions. The installation program will automatically copy all the necessary software onto your computer for you.

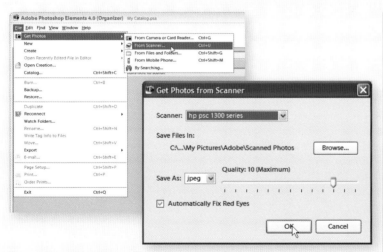

1 Open your image-editing software and you'll find that there will be an option that allows you to import images from your scanner. Here we're going to use Photoshop Elements, so choose *Get Photos > From Scanner*.

2 The software will automatically look for the scanner and its associated software and ask where you want the scan to be saved. More importantly it will also ask what quality you want the scan to be saved at—for our purposes always select "Maximum." Click *OK* and the scanner's software will launch.

3 Before starting the scanning process, select the type of image you're going to scan. Here we're scanning a faded color print, so select *Color picture*. If you want to scan what we usually refer to as a black-and-white photo, simply select *Grayscale picture*. You could even scan old documents by selecting *Black and white picture or text*. What Elements means by a "black-and-white" picture is a line drawing without any color or shades of gray.

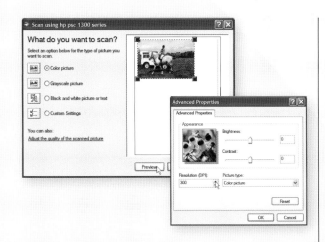

4 When you've selected the image type, press the *Preview* button. The scanner will make a quick pass over the image to identify its size. At this point you could adjust the bounding box so that only part of the image was scanned, we want the whole image, however. Before continuing with the scan, check that you're happy with the resolution that the scanner will scan at. With Elements, click *Adjust the quality of the scanned picture* to take you to the *Advanced Properties* box.

5 As this is a color picture that will be printed at a later stage, set *Resolution* to 300dpi (dots per inch). This will provide a good-sized image file with plenty of detail in the picture. When you're happy with the advanced settings, click *OK* to return to the main scan window.

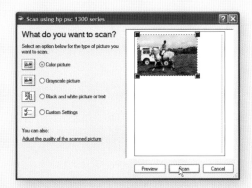

6 With all the settings verified, simply click *Scan* in the scanner's dialog window.

7 After a short while, depending on the size of the image that you are scanning and the resolution that it is being scanned at, the scan will complete and open in a new window in Photoshop Elements.

SCANNER RESOLUTION

When scanning photographs, you will be asked at what resolution you'd like your image to be scanned. Resolution figures in the digital world vary enormously from device to device and are often very confusing.

For scanning photographs that will be printed at the same size, the rule of thumb is to use a resolution of 300dpi. If you're scanning something that will be printed at twice the size of the original, use 600dpi. However, if you are scanning a photo that will reduce in size when printed, you should still scan at 300dpi—you can always reduce it in your photoediting software. Finally, if you're scanning an image to be used on the Internet, you only really need to scan at 50–72dpi; however, you never know when you may need a print of the image, so you should scan at 300dpi and optimize (prepare for the Web) the image in your editing software.

fixing faded images

One of the most common problems with both color and black-and-white images, particularly those that have been exposed to sunlight for long periods of time, is that they will fade. However, most image-editing software is capable of extracting the remnants of the color left in a color print, or bringing back the tone in a black-and-white photo.

Boosting Color

3 The *Hue and Saturation* dialog features a helpful before and after window of the image and three sliders. The one that will help bring back the color to the image is the *Saturation* slider. Increase the *Saturation* value until the preview window begins to show a more colorful image.

1 This image is typical of an old color photo that has been exposed to daylight for many years. Fortunately, the colors appear to have faded uniformly and there is little evidence of color change. This makes it easier to simply boost the existing colors.

2 For this example, we'll use Ulead PhotoImpact's *Hue and Saturation* command to boost the colors. This is a common editing feature found in most image-editing software, and all of the packages work in much the same way. With PhotoImpact, go to *Photo > Color > Hue and Saturation* to bring up the *Hue and Saturation* dialog window.

4 And here's the result; a very quick and easy way to bring back some of that missing color.

Improving Tone

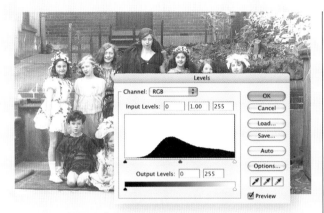

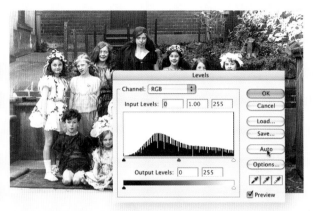

1 In this example, we'll bring back some of the original tone to this faded, yet emotive black-and-white print using Elements.

2 The best way to fix this type of problem is to bring up the image-editing software's *Levels* command. Go to *Enhance > Adjust Lighting > Levels*. As you can see from the histogram— a diagrammatic representation of the image's tonal values—there is very little information on the left-hand side, which represents the darker tones of the image.

3 By clicking *Auto* in the *Levels* dialog window, Elements automatically arranges the tones of the image's pixels so that there is a more even spread from pure black to pure white. The result is a much punchier image with stronger blacks.

4 To make the image appear even less dated and faded, simply desaturate the image of all its color by going to *Enhance > Adjust Color > Remove Color*.

fixing damaged photos

Photographs deteriorate rapidly if they are carelessly handled or improperly stored. We've looked at how to improve faded images, but what about images that are blemished, scratched, or even torn? Fixing such images is possible, but requires patience, time, and a good understanding of how your image-editing repair tools work.

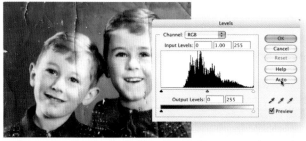

2 First, as before, bring back a complete tonal range to the image. Call up the *Levels* command and click *Auto*. Although this makes the image look less faded, it emphasizes the damage that the photo has sustained. The tears and creases appear deeper and the spots and scratches more numerous— but they've all got to be fixed anyway.

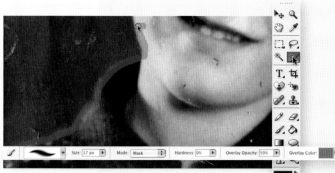

1 This portrait of two young brothers is badly damaged. It's faded, there are bad tears and scratches, and—most difficult of all to repair—deep creases running down both their faces. Before scanning the image, a very lightweight tape was stuck to the back to hold the torn sections together. Make sure you don't use a tape that will rip the back of the picture when you remove it after scanning. Also, avoid leaving sticky tape on an old print for any length of time because it may degrade the paper. We'll use Photoshop Elements to carry out this restoration.

3 The next thing is to isolate the boys from the background. That way we can fix the background quickly and easily without any time-consuming, click-by-click repair work. Choose the *Selection Brush* tool from the *Toolbar*, and ensure that its *Mode* is set to *Mask* in the *Tool Options* bar. While here, select a small soft brush—the default red *Overlay Color* and 50 percent *Overlay Opacity* is fine for this job. Begin by carefully painting a mask around the outer edge of the boys.

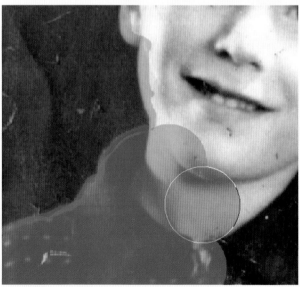

4 When you've completed the outline of the boys, change to a larger brush and fill in the outline. To change the size of the brush use the "[" and "]" keys—it saves having to go to the *Tool Options* bar each time.

5 Once you've completed the mask go to *Select > Feather* and enter a *Feather Radius* of 4 pixels. This will help soften the outline of the boys from the background.

fixing damaged photos continued

6 Now, with the *Selection Brush* tool still selected, go to the *Tool Options* bar and change the *Mode* to *Selection*. You will now have the background selected.

7 Duplicate the background by going to *Layer > New > Layer via Copy*. In the *Layers* palette you'll see a new layer; call it "Background 2."

8 With "Background 2" selected, move the cursor onto the thumbnail image in the *Layers* palette and, while holding down the Ctrl key (Cmd on a Mac), click the mouse to load the selection—the bounding box (or "marching ants") will reappear around the boys in the main window.

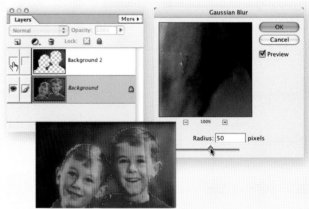

9 Click on the visibility eye on the "Background 2" layer to render that layer invisible. Return to the first "Background" layer and go to *Filter > Blur > Gaussian Blur* and enter a *Radius* value of 50. This nearly fixes the tears and scratches in the background while retaining the image's light and shade. There will, however, be one or two places where the worst-offending scratches and tears are visible.

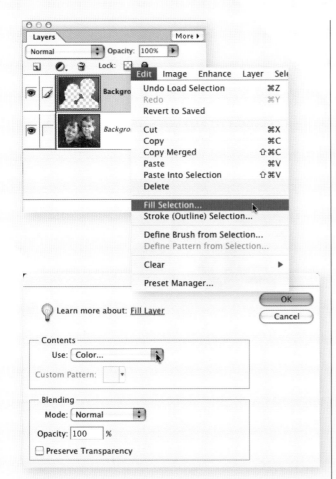

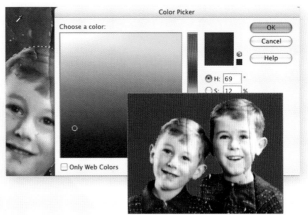

11 When the *Color Picker* dialog box appears, move the cursor over the image—the cursor will turn into the *Eyedropper* tool. Select a point in the background and you'll notice the *Color Picker* will match the color. Click *OK* and the background will be filled with the color. At the moment, the result looks flat and unreal.

10 To fix these and to give the blurred background some substance, return to the "Background 2" layer—the original damaged background will reappear along with the selection around the boys. Go to *Edit > Fill* and select *Color* from the *Use* drop-down menu.

12 To bring back some of the light and shade from the original background, reduce the opacity of the "Background 2" layer using the *Opacity* slider. You should now see some of the blurred background showing through.

fixing damaged photos continued

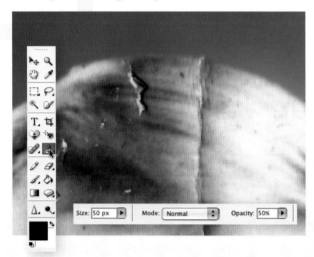

13 Now we'll tackle the larger scratches and creases, paying particular attention to those that affect the boys' heads and faces. Select the *Clone Stamp* tool from the *Toolbar*. Zoom right into an area that needs to be repaired and select an appropriately sized brush. Finally, set the *Opacity* to around 50 percent.

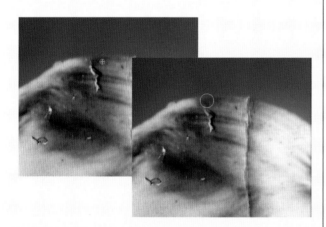

14 Place the cursor adjacent to a damaged area and hold down the Alt/Option key. The circle will turn into a target icon—this represents the source point. With the Alt/Option key held down, click the mouse and move the circle over to the point that you want to repair. Repeat this click-drag-click routine and the damaged area will slowly be replaced with the source point.

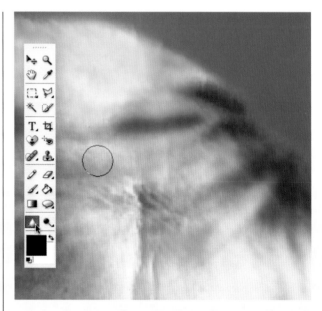

15 For the less-damaged areas, where the creasing is light, try using the *Blur* tool to "flatten" out the crease. The *Blur* tool is also a useful way to erase small repeated lines.

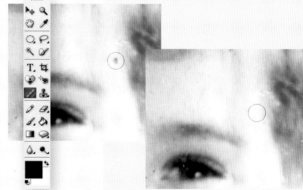

16 Once you've dealt with the major damage, it's time to clean up the smaller blemishes and spots. The ideal tool for this job is the *Spot Healing Brush* tool. Select the tool from the *Toolbar*, navigate to a spot that you want to erase, and use the "[" and "]" keys to size the brush so that it fits around the blemish. Next, simply click the mouse and the spot will vanish.

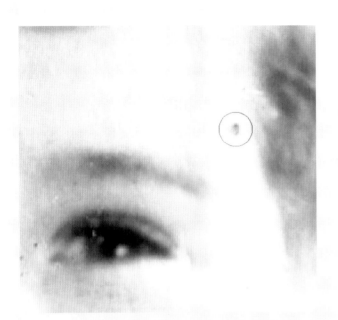

17 Finally, check for any other missed scratches, spots, and blemishes and fix those as described before.

UNDO HISTORY

It takes practice to get the repair to look natural, and you may find that an ugly repeat pattern emerges. If this happens, remember to vary the source point frequently. Remember also to use the *Undo* command (Ctrl/Cmd+Z) whenever you're not happy with a repair. Elements also features an *Undo History* palette that allows you to retrace your steps. Over time you'll become increasingly familiar with this tool.

18 If you want to bring back the slightly sepia effect that the original had, go to *Enhance > Adjust Color > Adjust Hue/Saturation*. In the *Hue/Saturation* dialog box, click the *Colorize* button, and adjust the *Hue* and Saturation sliders until you reach a tint that you're happy with.

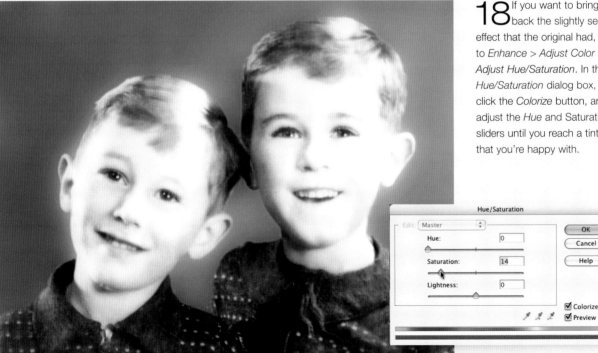

retouching portraits

There will be many occasions when, having taken a quick candid shot of a family member or friend, you find that the subject of the photo is not necessarily looking his or her best. The dilemma is that while you may end up with a photo that captures the essence or character of the subject because the shutter release was pressed just at the right time and caught a good natural expression, the subject may not feel happy with the shot because of skin blemishes or other problems.

Improving skin complexion and brightening eyes is quite a simple process in most image-editing software packages. In this project we're going to use the same tools that were used to fix the damaged photo; however, you need to be very careful when using these tools and methods to avoid your result looking artificial.

1 This photo of a young family member was taken on a dry, sunny, but windy day near the beach, and his skin looks very dry in places. He was also suffering from a cold at the time, and the area under his nose looks a little sore. But the expression and direct gaze are very natural and the slight backlighting captures the sunny day nicely.

2 The best tool in Photoshop Elements to improve skin complexion and fix the areas of dry skin is the *Clone Stamp*. We're dealing with very delicate areas, where the slightest change can dramatically alter the photo, so select a very low *Opacity* percentage—here we've used 10 percent.

9 px   Mode: Normal   Opacity: 10%   ☑ Aligned

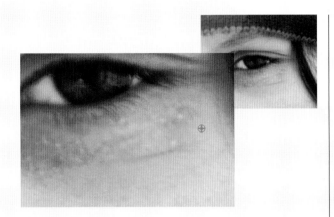

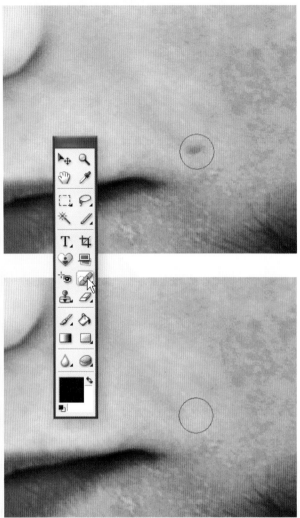

3 Begin by using the *Zoom* tool to zoom in close on an area that you want to improve. Select the *Clone Stamp* tool with a low *Opacity*. As you move the cursor over the image area, hold down the Alt key (Opt on a Mac) key and the circle will turn into a target symbol. Place the target over an area you want to use as the cloning source. This should match as closely as possible the skin tone and color of the skin you want to improve.

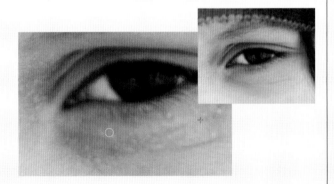

4 When you're happy with the clone source, click and release the mouse to "load" the source, and then move to an area that needs to be improved. Carefully brush over the offending area. You'll notice a small cross mirroring the moves made by the *Clone Stamp* tool. This indicates the pixels that are being used to make the repair. To achieve a natural-looking result, change the source of the *Clone Stamp* tool regularly; you may find that changing the size of the brush (using the "[" and "]" keys) also helps. Once you've been around the entire face fixing the dry skin, it's time to move to the next stage.

5 More localized areas such as freckles or pimples are easily fixed using the *Spot Healing* tool. Simply select the tool, place the tool's circle over the spot and, again using the "[" and "]" keys, size the tool so that it fits neatly over the spot. Next simply click the mouse and the blemish will disappear, to be replaced by a patch of clear skin.

retouching portraits continued

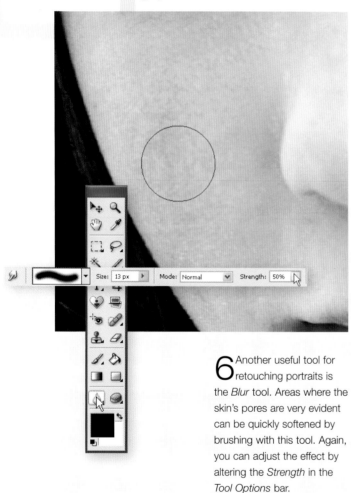

7 With careful use of the *Clone Stamp*, *Spot Healing*, and *Blur* tools the boy's skin now appears much smoother and clearer, but not unnatural. We could leave the portrait at this stage, but there are one or two other things that may enhance it even further.

6 Another useful tool for retouching portraits is the *Blur* tool. Areas where the skin's pores are very evident can be quickly softened by brushing with this tool. Again, you can adjust the effect by altering the *Strength* in the *Tool Options* bar.

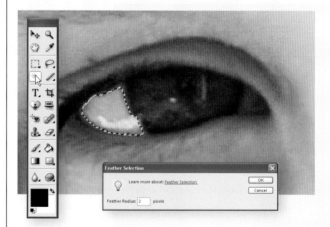

8 Here we'll lighten the whites of the eyes very slightly. Begin by zooming into one of the eyes. Select the *Magic Wand* tool from the *Toolbar* and click in a white area of the eye. When you're happy with the selection go to *Select > Feather* and enter a *Feather Radius* of 2 pixels. This softens the edges of the selection so that the whiter area spreads softly rather than stopping abruptly.

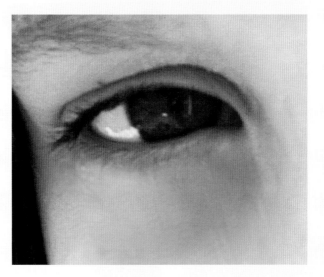

9 With the white of the eye selected, go to *Enhance > Adjust Lighting > Levels* (or use the keyboard shortcut Ctrl/Cmd+L) to bring up the *Levels* dialog box. To brighten the white, slide the middle slider to the left. If you find it hard to gauge the effect accurately because of the "marching ants" selection, press Ctrl/Cmd+H to hide them. Use the same combination to bring the marching ants back. Move the slider very carefully and return to a full view before committing to the change. When you're happy with one eye, make a note of the central input level—here it's 1.15. Move on to the next eye and enter the same value in the central input box. You want to make sure the change is almost imperceptible. If it's noticeable it won't look natural.

retouching portraits continued

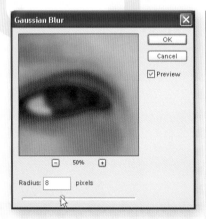

10 Create a new layer (*Layer > New > Layer*) and call it "Blur." Next go to *Filter > Blur > Gaussian Blur* and in the resulting *Gaussian Blur* dialog window enter a *Radius* of between 6 and 8 pixels. This will result in a very blurred image, so return to the *Layers* palette and reduce the *Opacity* of the "Blur" layer to around 50 percent. This reduces the effect of the *Gaussian Blur* filter to give a soft-focus result.

11 To bring life back to the eyes and any other areas of the face, simply select the *Eraser* tool from the *Toolbar* and, with the "Blur" layer selected, erase the eyes and the mouth. This instantly sharpens those areas. If you check the "Blur" layer thumbnail in the *Layers* palette you can immediately see those areas that have been erased, leaving the sharper "Background" layer to show through.

12 To finish the retouching go to *Layer > Flatten Image*. This version of the image has a very slight soft-focus effect, but the eyes are still sharp enough to hold the gaze.

TAKING IT FARTHER

To create a fashion-style image, try desaturating the colors a little by going to *Enhance > Adjust Color > Adjust Hue/Saturation* and reducing the *Saturation*. Then duplicate the "Background" image as before, but try experimenting with various blending modes; here we used *Screen* to create a high-key photo effect.

banishing red eye

The dreaded red-eye effect has been the bane of amateur photographers' lives since the invention of the built-in flash. Caused by the sudden bright light of the camera's flash reflecting off the back of the subject's eyes and through the enlarged pupils at the front, red eye must be responsible for ruining hundreds of millions of photographs over the years—with much loved grandchildren turning into instant horror figures. If the eyes are the windows to the soul, then red probably isn't the color that you want to see in them.

It is for exactly this reason that image-editing software developers have spent a lot of time devising ways of making it as easy as possible to fix this problem; since despite the invention of the red eye reduction light—a little lamp at the front of the camera that lights up a fraction before the flash fires in order to reduce the pupil size—red eye is still a common fault.

Ulead PhotoImpact

1 Here's a typical red-eye shot. Having spent ages persuading these two to actually sit next to each other (let alone hug each other) before taking the photo, the result is far from ideal and still not suitable for e-mailing to doting grandparents.

2 Using Ulead PhotoImpact, select the *Remove Red Eye* tool from the *Toolbar*, and then zoom in close to one of the offending eyes.

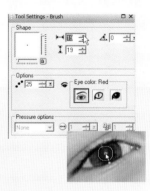

3 In the *Brush Tool Settings* palette use the various controls to adjust the size of the brush so that it fits neatly over the red area of the eye (this usually equates to the pupil). Notice that PhotoImpact also features yellow and green eye removal options for the pets of the house.

4 Click with the *Brush* tool over the red element of the eye and the red will begin to be replaced by black. Keep clicking until you are happy with the result. Continue with this, adjusting the brush size as necessary until all the eyes have been corrected.

Photoshop Elements

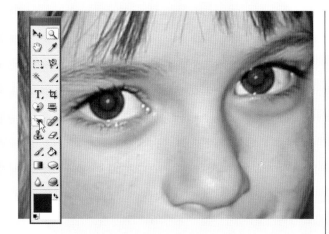

1 Using Elements to fix red eye is just as simple, if not more so. Begin by selecting the *Red Eye Removal* tool from the *Toolbar* and using the *Zoom* tool, zoom in close to the eyes.

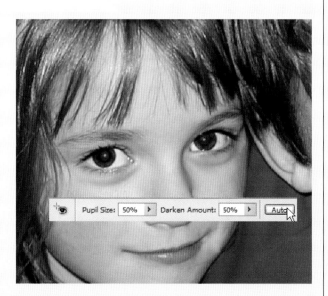

2 In the *Tool Options* bar, leave both *Pupil Size* and *Darken Amount* at 50 percent, and click *Auto*. Elements automatically looks for the red eye in the picture and fixes it.

3 You can have more control over the process. With the *Red Eye Removal* tool selected, move the cursor (which will take the form of a small cross) on to the center of the eye and simply click once, before moving on to the next eye.

4 With all four pupils returned to their natural black, the image is now ready to send.

fixing color casts

An unnatural-looking color bias in a photograph, known as a color cast, can be caused by a variety of factors. Old photographs that have been exposed to sunlight for many years can fade and, worse, take on an unpleasant-looking reddish or yellow color. Once this has happened to the photo, there's not much that can be done other than to scan it and try to fix the digital file in photoediting software.

Color casts are also caused by strong natural light, such as the warming and acceptable reds from a tropical sunrise, or by artificial light, such as the less-acceptable blues caused by fluorescent lights. To counteract this, digital cameras have white-balance settings that help the image retain natural colors. However, the white-balance setting doesn't always get things right, and often you'll find images with an unsightly color cast. Fixing discolored digital image files, whether from a digital camera or a scanner, is usually achievable with most image-editing software.

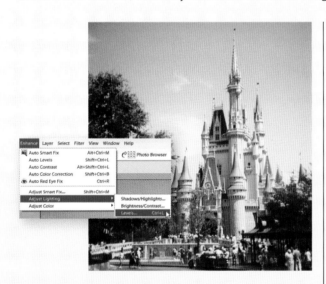

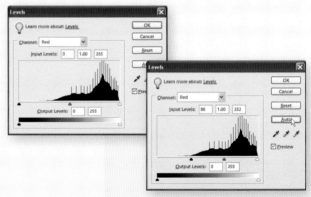

1 This photograph is almost 25 years old, and its exposure to daylight has caused it to take on an unnatural-looking red-pink color.

2 Select the *Levels* command in your image-editing software; we're using Photoshop Elements here, so go to *Enhance > Adjust Lighting > Levels*; use the Ctrl+L (Cmd+L on a Mac) keys to bring up the *Levels* dialog window. It's useful to try to remember these "keyboard shortcuts"—they become second nature after you've been using them for a while, and they can save a surprising amount of time and effort.

3 Although we normally think of *Levels* as a brightness adjustment tool that is used to fix underexposed or overexposed images, *Levels* can also be used to fix color casts. You'll notice that in the dialog window next to *Channel* are the letters *RGB*. These stand for Red, Green, and Blue, the primary colors that go to make up all the colors in the digital image. If you click on the drop-down menu, you'll find that you can select any one of these channels and adjust it independently of the other colors. If you look at the *Red* channel you'll notice how all the reds are grouped up on the right side of the histogram (the black graph that represents the images tones). Click *Auto* and the left-hand (black point) triangle moves to sit under the left edge of the histogram. This gives the red pixels a much more even tonal spread. Apply this to all the colors by returning to the *RGB* channel and clicking *Auto*.

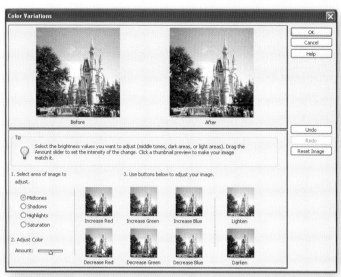

4 The result is quite a drastic improvement. The red color cast has all but disappeared and the other colors are much more evident. However, look carefully at the trees and the Disney castle and you'll still notice a slight pink tinge.

5 To fix this, use another of Photoshop Elements' color-correction tools. Go to *Enhance > Adjust Color > Color Variations* to bring up the *Color Variations* dialog window. This is a very simple, but very powerful tool. To dispense with the pink color cast once and for all, click on the *Decrease Red* window. The *After* preview window shows a much more accurate image.

6 The final result reflects the *Color Variations* preview window. The red color cast has now entirely disappeared. The trees are a much healthier green and the fairyland castle a purer white.

sharpening images

Sometimes, having scanned a photo or downloaded one from your digital camera and opened it on the computer, you may notice that the image looks a little blurred or "soft." This softness can be improved by using image-editing software. Although. if a photo is actually out of focus then, unfortunately, there is little that can be done.

Images from scanners and digital cameras can occasionally appear soft because of the internal processing the image undergoes within the device or due to the file format in which the image is saved. Furthermore, some scanners provide various settings for sharpening images using their own internal sharpening software. Be wary of these, particularly when scanning, as you're likely to get much better results using your image-editing software to sharpen the image after it's been scanned.

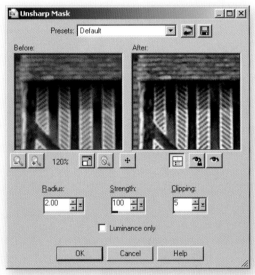

1 This image, although by no means out of focus, is definitely "soft." Using Paint Shop Pro it will be quite straightforward to bring out a bit more detail in the buildings.

2 Begin the sharpening process by going to *Adjust > Sharpness > Unsharp Mask*. Paint Shop Pro is not unique in having an *Unsharp Mask* command. Photoshop Elements and Ulead's PhotoImpact, to name just two other editing programs, also feature this powerful sharpening tool.

3 Having brought up the *Unsharp Mask* dialog window, select Paint Shop Pro's default sharpening settings as shown here. The *Unsharp Mask* comprises three settings; *Radius*, *Strength* (or *Amount*), and *Clipping* (or *Threshold*). The two key controls are *Radius* and *Strength*. The *Unsharp Mask* works by finding the edges in an image and increases the contrast either side of the edge, creating a halo effect that simulates sharper edges. The *Radius* setting defines the thickness of the halos, the *Strength* setting determines the amount to which the image's edges are sharpened, while *Clipping*, depending on its value, includes or excludes pixels to be sharpened.

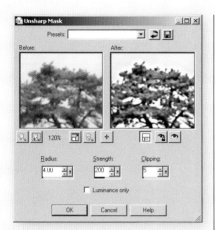

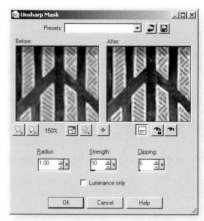

4 Here, the *Radius* setting has been increased to 4 and the *Strength* to 200 to show how the *Unsharp Mask* works. The halo effect discussed earlier is clearly apparent, particularly around the edges of the trees, and the image is now what is termed "oversharpened." Let's return to the default settings.

5 Even at the default settings of *Radius*: 2, *Strength*: 100 and *Clipping*: 5 there is still a faint halo effect around the tree. It's areas such as these, with a uniform background color such as the sky, that are most prone to the halo effect. So check these areas before finalizing the *Unsharp Mask* values.

6 By reducing the *Radius* to 1, the *Strength* to 90, and increasing the *Clipping* to 6 (which excludes a few more pixels from the sharpening effect) the halo around the tree has gone, but as the close up of the herringbone pattern on the building shows, there is a definite sharpening effect.

7 Comparing the start image and the final image here shows how the *Unsharp Mask* has removed the softness to the image and brought out more detail.

slide shows

Viewing your images as a professional-looking slide show is a great way to enjoy your photographs. And once you've created the slide show you'll discover that you aren't restricted to watching it only on your computer screen—Elements also enables you to send the slide show to your television to view it there, create a disc to send to family and friends for them to watch, and, if you have access to e-mail, even send it to distant relatives on the other side of the world.

In the following project we will also be looking at how you can add text, music, and borders to your slide show, giving an even more professional look and feel.

Unfortunately not all photoediting programs have the ability to create slide shows, so you'll need to check in your editing software's manual whether or not it's possible. Photoshop Elements, however, is able to create shows, and the program provides help along the way.

1 When you first open Photoshop Elements, the welcome screen shows you various options. Click on *Make Photo Creations*, which includes the *Make slideshows with music and narration* option among others. If you don't see the welcome screen, click the *Create* button in the menu bar.

2 In the resulting *Creation Setup* window, select *Slide Show* and then click *OK*.

3 Before Elements creates the slide show, you'll be shown a *Slide Show Preferences* dialog box. It's probably a good idea at this stage to stick with the default options until you become more familiar with how the slide show works. Once you've viewed the slide show with the default settings a few times, you'll be in a better position to judge if you'd like to alter anything. All that we've done here is checked the *Apply Pan & Zoom to All Slides* box.

4 The next step is to open the images you want to include in the slide show. If you've already used Elements and know that your images are in the *Organizer* go to *Add Media > Photos and Videos from Organizer*. If, however, you're importing your images from another folder on your computer, select *Photos and Videos from Folder*, navigate to the folder where your images are stored, and click *Open*.

5 Elements will then automatically open the *Slide Show Editor*, where you'll see all the imported images running in a Timeline at the bottom of the screen; here, each slide will show for 5 seconds before the transition to the next slide begins. Filling the main window will be the first image of your selection. To see the slide show run within the main screen click the forward arrow underneath the main image. If you click the *Preview* button to the top-right of the window, the slide show runs without the various tools, options, and menus around it.

Slide Shows continued

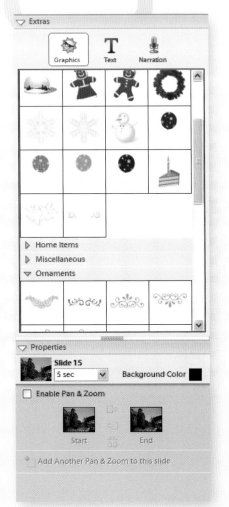

6 The *Slide Show Editor* features a range of options. The most important are the *Extras* and *Properties* palettes. Clicking on the *Graphics* button within the *Extras* palette will present you with a wide range of colored artworks for a variety of occasions such as birthdays, vacations, and so on, as well as folders containing borders that you can drag onto a slide and position where you like. The *Properties* palette allows you to edit all or individual slides. For example, you can extend the time the slides are shown or change the background color.

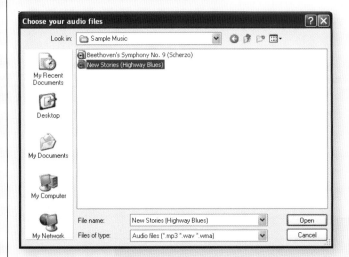

7 To add a soundtrack to the show, click the *Add Media* button as before, and again, depending on where you've stored your audio tracks, navigate to the relevant folder, select the track, and click *Open*.

8 Elements will now import the audio files into the *Slide Show Editor*, where they'll appear beneath the thumbnail images in the timeline. Because you're using the default settings, the selected audio track(s) will repeat until the end of the slide show, as indicated.

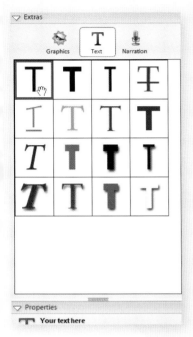

9 To add text to any of your slides, use the timeline and click on the slide that you want to add text to. Next, click on *Text* in the top menu of the *Extras* palette, and then simply click the style of text that you want to add to the slide.

11 An *Edit Text* dialog window will now appear, into which you can type the text that you want to appear on the slide. Once you're happy with the text, click *OK*.

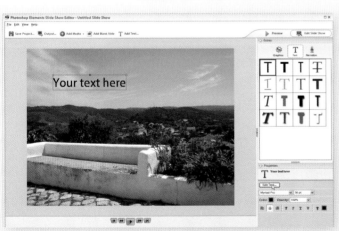

10 Drag the "T" of your chosen text style onto the slide image. Elements will automatically create a text box with the words "Your text here." Now click the *Edit Text* box in the *Properties* palette.

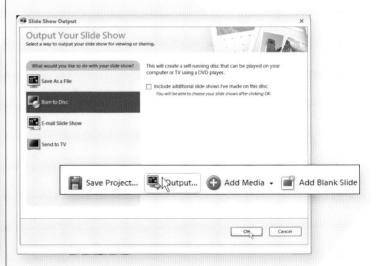

12 After you've previewed your slide show, made any changes, and are happy with the result, go to *Output* in the menu bar. You'll then be taken to the *Slide Show Output* options window. Here you'll be presented with four options. Whichever option you select, Elements will show you how to complete the outputting of your slide show.

saving photos for the Web

There are an increasing number of companies that, for a small fee or even for free, will provide you with space on the Internet where you can put your images for anyone who knows the website address to view. This is an easy and efficient way to show your images to anyone in the world—all you need to do is give them the website details; so there's no need to e-mail your images time and again to individual people.

The file sizes for images viewed on a computer screen can be much smaller than those images that are intended for print, this is because a computer screen has much lower resolution than a printed image. However, because it's good practice to scan images or set your digital camera at a resolution high enough to print if you ever need to, it's necessary to reduce the file size of your photos before putting them on the Web. Some cameras can produce file sizes of over 20 megabytes, which would take even the fastest Internet connection an extremely long time to download. To reduce the file size you need to "optimize" your images.

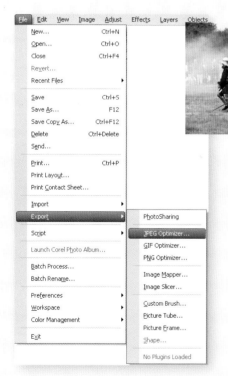

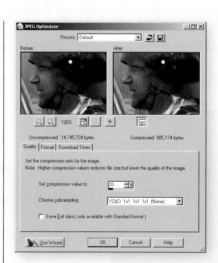

1 The file size of this image of an English Civil War reconstruction is almost 15 megabytes (MB), which is far too big to load onto the Web for general use, so it needs to come down a lot in size.

2 Using Paint Shop Pro, start the image optimization process by going to *Export > JPEG Optimizer*. Other software will have a slightly different name for the same option, such as *Save for Web*, but it should be fairly obvious which menu option you need.

3 When Paint Shop Pro opens the *JPEG Optimizer* window, you get confirmation about the original image's file size. Selecting *Default* from the *Presets* option in Paint Shop Pro sets a compression value of 20. Compressing works by replacing pixels of a similar color and tone with one big block of that color and tone so less information is need to show the same area of the image. With compression set to 20 the *After* preview window looks pretty good—there's no real discernible drop in image quality, and the file is now less than 1 megabyte—a sizeable reduction from the original. As rule, leave the *Chroma subsampling* untouched.

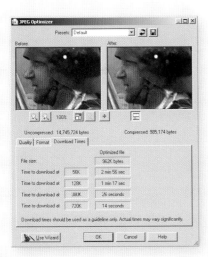

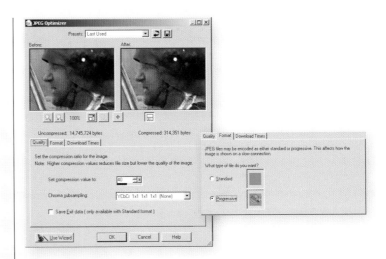

4 Click on the *Download Times* tab and you'll see that a file that size is going to take even the fastest connection 14 seconds to download and the slowest, which is a typical dial-up connection, a lengthy 3 minutes. Few people can wait that long.

6 Return to the *Quality* window and set the compression to 40. In the *Format* window you'll see two options, *Standard* and *Progressive*. In *Standard* mode the image won't appear until it has completely downloaded, but in *Progressive* mode a low-resolution image will quickly appear, getting more detailed as the file loads.

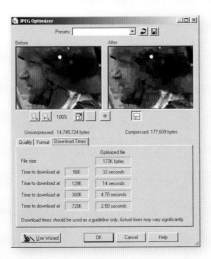

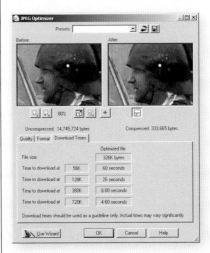

5 Return to the *Quality* window and increase the compression to around 80. Now when looking in the *Download Times* window you can see the download time is much more acceptable, but, unfortunately, the quality of the image has dropped quite considerably; in fact, it's no longer acceptable. And this is the crux of optimizing images—trading off download times with image quality.

7 Finally, check on the *Download Times* and the *Quality*. The slowest time is down to just under a minute, which is still a long time, but a great improvement, while the fastest time is down to around 4 seconds. Checking in the *After* preview window shows that the image is of a sufficient quality. The image is now ready to upload to the website.

e-mailing photos

Millions of people around the world now have their own e-mail accounts, sending messages via e-mail is a daily occupation for most of us, whether at home or at work. And because all our e-mails are sent via local computer networks, it costs exactly the same to send an e-mail to someone the other side of the world as it does to send one to someone on the other side of the street.

But it's not just messages that can be sent via e-mail, it's also a convenient, cost effective, and extremely quick way of sending photographs as well—and today's image-editing software applications have made sending images an almost one-click operation.

Close All	⌥⌘W
Save	⌘S
Save As...	⇧⌘S
Save for Web...	⌥⇧⌘S
Attach to Email...	
Create Web Photo Gallery...	

1 This photograph taken at a steam engine show needed to be sent to someone over e-mail so that they could use it as a reference for a painting.

2 In Photoshop Elements all that is required is to select the *Attach to E-mail* icon in the menu bar, or go to *File > Attach to Email*.

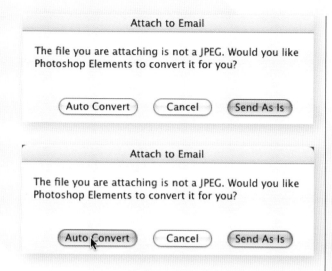

1 Ulead's PhotoImpact software works in very much the same way. Either select the *Send* icon in the menu bar, or go to *File > Export > Send*.

3 Helpfully, Elements assesses the file that's being sent, and a warning message appears if it's over a certain size, asking if you want Elements to reduce the size of the file before sending it or not. It's usually a safer option to select *Auto Convert*.

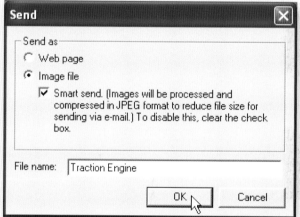

2 Like Elements, PhotoImpact will automatically reduce the image file's size and save it as a JPEG (if the image is not already in that format) should you want it to.

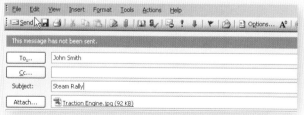

4 Once Elements has finished converting the file to an appropriate size, it will automatically launch the e-mail program ready for you to fill in the contact details, add any necessary subject message, and then send.

3 And again like Elements, once the file has been reformatted and reduced in size, PhotoImpact will automatically launch the preferred e-mail software.

section two
video

converting old film

The thought of inserting an expensive roll of film into a cine camera for the benefit of three minutes of home-movie footage that then needs to be sent away for processing before it can be viewed seems a rather quaint and somewhat impractical one in this digital age. However, roll back the clock thirty years or more and that's what home movie making was all about. Although an expensive hobby by today's standards, it's perhaps surprising to discover that there remains a considerable amount of cine film awaiting conversion to a digital form. In the late '60s and '70s, the most popular format was Super8, which is still used by some die-hard filmmakers to this day. Before that, Standard 8mm

was used in addition to its professional cousin, 16mm. If you need to copy cine film onto video, you'll require some specialized equipment. Of course, having a projector in the appropriate format helps. If you have rolls of Super8 film and the projector to play them on, you're halfway there.

Optical transfers

The quickest way to copy film to video is to point a video camera at the projection screen and (if appropriate) take an audio line output from the projector and connect it to the camcorder's audio input. There are better ways to achieve this, and a look through a local services directory will probably lead you to specialist

Right Project the film onto a small reflective white area. High gloss inkjet printer paper is ideal for this purpose.

companies who can undertake what's called a "telecine" transfer. Here's the do-it-yourself approach, however.

The first thing you need to do is to set the projector up so that it can project a clear picture onto a bright white, highly reflective surface. Aim to create a small image—one that occupies a piece of letter-sized paper will suffice, as this concentrates the light. "High Gloss" inkjet printer paper is good for this purpose. Now set up your camcorder on a tripod, positioned so that it looks over the projector in such a way as to minimize image distortion.

Manual adjustments of exposure and white balance

With the camcorder set in its most suitable position, put the camcorder into Record Standby mode and run the film. View it in the camcorder's LCD screen— or, better still, on a TV screen, using the camcorder's supplied AV output cables. What you'll now see won't impress you, but there are adjustments you can make to improve things.

The first thing you'll notice is that the picture will bleach out on the bright sections, and it will quite possibly have a yellow/green hue. It's really important to switch off auto controls and use manual adjustments throughout. Firstly, lock the camcorder's focus at a point where the film image is sharp, and then set the white balance as follows. Run the film out of the project to the point where the projector light throws only a white image onto the card. Now set the white balance ("WB") manually—referring to the user guide in order to check the procedure if necessary.

Once this has been done, ensure that the exposure is set to an optimum level by running the film and making the appropriate adjustments until you're reasonably happy with the results.

Overcoming frame flicker

Super8 cine film will have been exposed at 16 frames per second (fps), 18fps, or even (in the case of sound film recordings) 24fps. Each and every one of these will cause a flicker on the video picture, something that you'll not be able to eliminate completely. If your camcorder has an electronic shutter utility, experiment with settings for best results. Once you're happy, start recording!

converting VHS and Video8

Above Remember that you'll never improve on the original tape quality, so take care of your recordings and use the best player possible for optimum transfer quality.

We all have many VHS tape recordings that are worth transferring into the digital domain, and with both manufacturers and retailers now turning their backs on the analog video recording format altogether, it's an appropriate time to think about how to copy those cherished recordings onto computer and—ultimately—to DVD. It could be that you also have a selection of camcorder recordings made not only in VHS but also Video8, Hi8, or even Betamax. The principle for converting these analog formats to digital is identical.

Using a digital camcorder's AV-input capability

It's a little-known fact that many DV, DVD, and Digital8 camcorders can also be used as digital video recorders. In addition to the standard digital output and input connector called FireWire, or i.Link in some cases, all camcorders will have connections enabling you to play your recordings out to TV or recorder.

This is called an AV output connection. However, your camcorder may allow you to record back to digital tape or disk in the camcorder via this socket, too. This is called AV-in, and makes it very easy for you to connect a VHS player, camcorder or other device and copy older recordings to the camcorder. Simply press *Play* on the VHS player, hit *Record* on the camcorder and your recordings have been converted to digital.

Using pass-through

Some camcorders will not only allow an AV-input to tape or disk, but will also allow that signal to be passed directly to a Windows PC or Apple Mac computer via the FireWire connector without first re-recording. This AV pass-through recording is very useful—especially when you have large amounts of footage to be digitized and have limited time in which to do it. Normally, only tape-based formats like DV and Digital8 camcorders can be used in this way, since DVD, HDD (hard disk drive), and solid-state SD (secure digital) Card cameras use a different type of digital recording format.

Using an AV converter device

There are several dedicated devices that will allow you to connect the analog video and audio cables from a VHS player or camcorder at one end and then send a digital conversion signal to a computer via FireWire at the other end. Popular makes include Canopus, Miglia, and Datavideo. They perform the same function as a camcorder with pass-through conversion and are, of course, an additional expense. You don't need to tie up your camcorder for this purpose, however.

Composite and component

Look at the AV connecting cables that came with your camcorder and you'll see that you have a triple-cable set containing a yellow, red, and white lead. These carry the composite video (picture) and stereo (Right/Left) sound channels respectively. It's likely that these cables will all merge into one multiway plug that inserts into the AV socket on the camcorder. Consult your camcorder's manual as well as the manual for the VHS player to check precise connections.

If you want to copy recordings from an S-VHS player or Hi8 camcorder, then consider using a special connector called S-Video, which might also be included in the cables that came with your camcorder. S-Video processes S-VHS and Hi8 video signals differently in order to retain the higher quality on offer, though it has no advantage when used with ordinary video recordings.

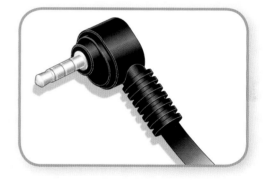

Above If you're copying from **S-VHS** or **Hi8** tapes, use an optional **S-Video** connector in place of the yellow composite video **RCA** plug for improved picture quality.

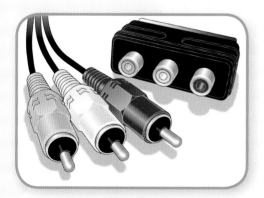

Left European readers will be familiar with the **SCART AV** adaptor plug. You'll need to acquire a switchable 2-way adaptor for copying analog tapes to your digital camcorder, however, as the supplied plugs are often only one-way.

Above A single AV multi-connector is often supplied with camcorders in order to provide easy output and input connections.

computer hardware

The favorite destination for digitized video recordings is undoubtedly DVD, although it's increasingly common for people to want to post snippets of home movies on their websites as well. Making a DVD recording of your cine films and analog video formats could be as easy as connecting a camcorder or AV converter into a stand-alone DVD recorder and simply pressing the *Record* button. However, for greater control and end-user interactivity it's still better to import all of your movies into a computer where you'll have many more creative and technical options.

Below Your computer monitor is a key part of your home video set up. Make sure it gives crisp graphics and good color reproduction. One reason why Apple Macs are favored by the graphics industry is that the Apple monitors that come with them have always been high quality.

What a computer needs for digital video

Computers designed to make the process of digital video editing and DVD creation have never been cheaper, with many systems now sold with this in mind. It doesn't matter whether you buy a Windows PC or Apple Mac computer—just check that the machine has a FireWire connection. This is also known as an i.Link or IEEE 1394 socket; other computer manufacturers call it a DV Link, but it's all the same thing.

Many digital camcorders now use USB 2.0 as the means to transfer video too, but almost all new computers will come with this connection. All modern Apple Mac computers, and most modern PCs, have both FireWire and USB 2.0 sockets, but it's worth double-checking with the vendor before you purchase. You'll also need to acquire the right kind of FireWire cable with which to connect the camcorder to the computer's FireWire socket. Note that there are two types of connector, a 4-pin plug and a larger 6-pin plug, so check carefully before purchasing a cable, because they're rarely included with new camcorders.

Using tapeless camcorders

Of course, an increasing number of camcorders don't use tape as the primary digital recording medium. DVD camcorders, for instance, are grabbing a large share of the market, as are cameras that use high-capacity hard disk drives (HDD) and also solid-state flash media cards, like SD-Video cams. Although the latter two formats are limited in terms of their digital conversion capabilities, many new DVD camcorders have analog video and audio inputs. To import the clips into the computer, you'll be able to either pop the disk into the computer's DVD drive, or copy the files across using the USB 2.0 connection. The type of compressed video—called MPEG2—isn't quite as good as DV and Digital8 tape, but it's a quick and easy way of achieving your aims.

Above You know when the computer has detected the camcorder's FireWire connection. iMovie's "Camera Connected" blue screen will confirm this. Windows PCs will produce a sound to confirm.

How to connect to the computer

Assuming your computer has the requisite FireWire connections (for DV and Digital8 tape camcorders, of course) and that you have the right FireWire cable, the job of transferring your movie clips is very simple once the connections have been made and tested.

With the camcorder in *Play* mode, connect the small FireWire plug into the camcorder (the socket will be called either DV, i.Link, or FireWire) and the other end

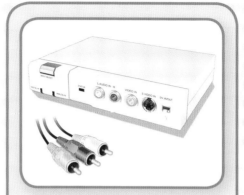

Although many digital camcorders will do the job effectively and economically, you may wish to utilise a standalone A-D (analog-to-digital) signal converter. Several products are available that are designed to accept analog inputs and then issue a digital signal conversion via FireWire that is then fed to the computer. All units facilitate a single-way conversion, but some devices will also perform conversions from and to analog. Such units are an additional expense, of course, but they save wear and tear on your digital camcorder.

into the computer's FireWire socket. The latter will be one of two types—a small 4-pin connection like that found on the camcorder, or a larger 6-pin socket such as those found on most computers. Once you've done this, you should hear a "bing-bong" sound on the computer (Windows PC), or see a notification appearing on-screen telling you that the camcorder has been connected. Often, the camcorder's LCD screen or viewfinder will display "DV-in" at this point, too.

Above and below Most computers rely on the larger 6-pin IEEE 1394 FireWire connectors, although many laptop PCs use the smaller 4-pin type as featured on camcorders. The type of 1394 FireWire cabling to connect your camcorder and computer will vary, but a single cable is all you need to carry all the signals.

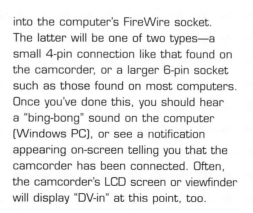

getting video into a computer

Although a stand-alone DVD recorder will enable you to make instant DVD recordings, complete with simple thumbnail-based menus making selection of movie clips very easy, it's in the computer that you have the greatest number of creative options for producing the perfect DVD or Web clip. What's more, the job of importing your video sequences into the computer, cutting out the rough bits, adding music and titles, and exporting the finished job to DVD is now very cheap. In fact, depending on the software choices you make, it needn't cost you a penny more that you paid for the computer!

Pre-installed digital video software

Whether you're a Windows PC or Apple Mac user, you'll be able to start editing your digital video movies right now, assuming you have the right hardware connections (see pages 48–49). All you need to start working with your video footage is some editing software. It may surprise you to know that you have instant access to one of two great pieces of software—Windows Movie Maker (PC) and iMovie (Apple Mac).

They're both exceedingly user-friendly, and aimed at beginners just like you. Even better—they're free, and pre-installed right there on your computer!

Although each of the programs has a unique look and feel, particularly in terms of the way the screen is laid out, they are each designed to do much the same job. The process of importing DV and Digital8 tape footage via FireWire is undertaken within the computer; with the camcorder connected, the software will take over the camcorder's functions and enable you to copy video clips onto the computer's internal hard-disk drive. You can do this clip by clip or simply "capture" the whole lot in one session.

Thumbnail images in the clip bin

The process of telling the program to copy your footage into the computer is as easy as clicking the mouse button, and when the video footage starts to copy you'll see little images (called "thumbnail icons") appearing in the window where the clips are stored. You'll also see that as each new clip starts, a new thumbnail

Right Windows Movie Maker contains very simple, standard capture tools for transferring video from your recorder to your computer.

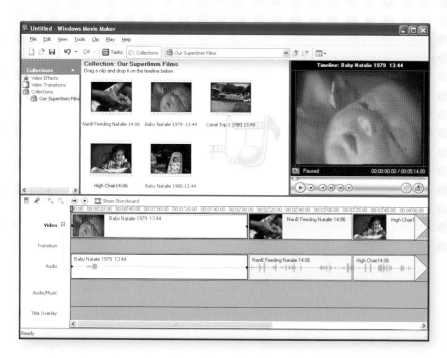

Left and below The Movie Maker screen is comprised of three main elements. The *Collections* window (often called the clip bin) contains the currently available clips. The preview window to the right allows you to preview either a single clip or the whole video. The timeline at the bottom is where the editing takes place, showing where clip a appears, how long it lasts, and whether it has a soundtrack.

is created, making it very easy for you to identify each clip. You can even give each clip a new name later. Once all of the video has been captured into the computer, the job of tidying up, reorganizing, and fine-tuning your movie is as quick as you'd want it to be.

Notice that the screen contains a window in which to view one or more clips. Simply click on one of the thumbnail icons and then on the "Play" control, and the selected clip will play with sound and vision. Do the same with another. Notice, also, that there's a linear section running across the bottom of the screen—this is called the timeline. The timeline is where you build up your movie by dragging individual clips from the clip bin to the timeline one at a time. Try it for yourself and you'll begin to see how easy it is! You can change the order of the clips by moving them at will. Remove a clip from the timeline (though not from your collection) by deleting it. That's it—you've discovered the joys of video editing!

video editing software

Right Although the design and layout of the editing interface varies, all beginner applications have much in common.

Once you've captured a selection of home movie clips in your computer, it's inevitable that you'll be thinking in terms of tidying up the sequences by cutting out the obviously bad bits, rearranging them, adding titles, music, and so on. That's where things really get exciting.

Although Windows Movie Maker and Apple iMovie might well satisfy your home video needs for some time to come, there's now a wide choice of low-cost digital video editing packages that you might also consider. These range from highly popular programs like Ulead's very successful Video Studio, to Pinnacle's own Studio series of low-cost programs.

Unlike Movie Maker and iMovie (which both rely on partner products to extend to disk-burning capabilities), these programs enable you to undertake the complete workflow—from initial capture to editing to DVD menu creation and burning of the disk. Another increasingly popular program is Adobe Premiere Elements, which possesses many of the on-screen characteristics and features of its professional big brother, Premiere Pro.

Common layout and functions
One thing that becomes apparent is that although all these programs have their own identifiable on-screen design and layout,

the actual screen components are very similar. It's just that things are in different places. All the programs have somewhere to display the available clips (the clip bin); they have a place to play a selected clip or sequence (the preview window) and a space in which to assemble the clips (the timeline) running along the bottom of the screen. It's on the timeline that the real creative stuff takes place, and where your movie project will be assembled.

Titles and music for that professional touch

Have a look at the examples on these pages and you'll see that the timeline is not only where your home movie video clips can be assembled—starting from the left and running to the right—but also where you can add titles, music, and effects. Additional tracks are provided in even the most basic applications, enabling you to build up a very professional-looking and sounding movie. Although each program differs slightly in terms of how these options are made available to you, you'll find that the ease with which you can actually progress from one to another means that the underlying functions and features are fairly common to all.

Moving, modifying, and deleting clips

As you arrange clips on the timeline, you'll discover that it's easy to drag them from one location to another to re-organise the order of clips in the sequence. You can trim the duration of a clip or—if it isn't up to your expectations—simply delete it from the sequence. Note that, in most cases, the clip won't be deleted forever, it's simply removed from the current timeline.

Above Windows Movie Maker refers to the part of the screen where your clips are stored as the Collections window. Apple's iMovie calls it the Clips pane. They each do the same job.

Above Users of Pinnacle Studio, a medium-price starter package, play clips in this Preview window. Note how playback can be manipulated with the use of simple control buttons that resemble those found on a standard VCR.

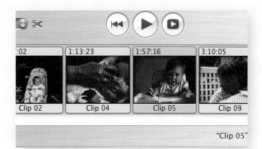

Left The timeline is where the clips are assembled and re-assembled after dragging them down from the clip bin. It's here that additional tracks are provided for the inclusion of music and effects, too.

splitting footage into scenes

Above Splitting a long clip into smaller segments is one of the easiest things to achieve in all editing applications. Select the point in the clip where you want to create the cut, and click the appropriate tool. In Movie Maker this is found immediately under the main preview window.

When you've been recording with a DV, Digital8, or other digital camcorder, a new clip will be started from each point where you pressed the *Record* button. Each time you did this, the camcorder saved some important information relating to the clip—called Metadata—onto the tape or disk. This data includes such information as the date and time the clip was recorded and the timecode point on the tape where it's saved. For DVD and tapeless formats, this data includes even more information relevant to the clip. When you record one long piece of cine film or VHS to tape or disk, this information is only created if you start and stop the recording at each new film roll or source tape. You may prefer to split the movie up yourself to make editing easier.

Trimming clips

All digital video editing programs make splitting clips very easy, and it's one of the most basic features of any such program. It's often not necessary to place clips down onto the timeline in order to modify the points at which they start and finish, either. Microsoft Windows Movie Maker allows you to move the playhead to the selected position where the *Split Clip* button is clicked. The clip will then be separated into two; this can be undertaken as many times as required.

Apple's iMovie is another program that makes it just as easy. The only difference is the way in which it's done. The whole point of this exercise is to shorten the clips in order to eliminate the excess material that you really don't want your viewers to have to watch. Whether your aim is to cut out the bits that are obviously no good, or to polish your movie work to a point where it has a professional look is really up to you. Whichever approach you follow, the tools exist in almost every program to enable you to achieve excellent results—even with those programs that come pre-installed with your computer hardware.

The *Crop* tool in iMovie is, for instance, a variation of similar tools that can be found in all the main digital video editing tools. By setting the new beginning and end points of a chosen clip, you're making a decision about what you want your viewers to see and what you don't want them to be exposed to. By combining this tool with the added ability to then rearrange the clip sequence, you're already engaged in the process of video editing, pure and simple.

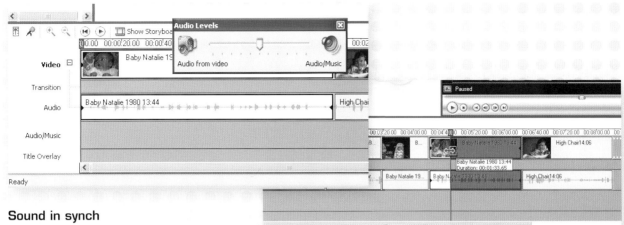

Sound in synch

Remember that in digitizing your old films and video recordings, you're likely to have transferred sound as well as moving pictures. The FireWire and USB 2.0 connections encode everything, and as you pull the clips into your project timeline you'll notice that the audio part of the timeline (the audio tracks that run in parallel to the video track containing your video clips) contains squiggly lines that represent the constantly changing sound tracks, known as the Audio Waveform. In the case of cine film, it's highly likely that your footage will be silent, but with copies of old VHS sequences you'll almost certainly be editing sound at the same time as pictures.

Be careful not to edit only the pictures. While trimming a clip at given points might make sense from a visual point of view, it could create confusion if you choose to cut in the middle of somebody speaking. It's important to listen carefully to the accompanying sound in order to determine its relevance to the pictures—and it might be indispensable. The waveform helps in this respect, as does Movie Maker's *Audio Mixer* control, which enables you to balance the camcorder's sound track with any additional music or effects you might choose to add later.

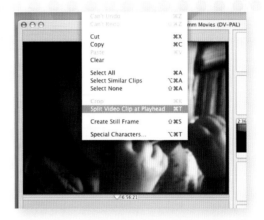

Top Unless they're silent, all clips contain synchronous sound that displays as a waveform, making editing and sound balancing much easier.

Above In most cases, the beginning and end of a clip can be trimmed by simply clicking on it and dragging the bar. Movie Maker makes this very easy.

Above-left With the clip playing in iMovie's preview window, select *Edit > Split Video Clip at Playhead*. The clip is now divided into two.

Left You can trim the beginning and end of a clip using iMovie's *Crop* tool. Drag each of the two tiny arrows under the preview window to the end and start points respectively, then select *Edit > Crop* in the toolbar.

re-editing material

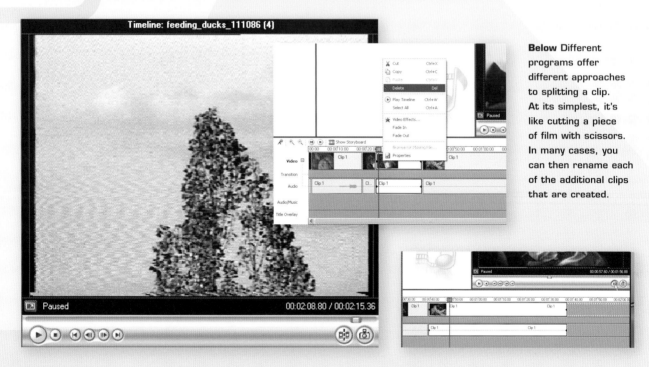

Below Different programs offer different approaches to splitting a clip. At its simplest, it's like cutting a piece of film with scissors. In many cases, you can then rename each of the additional clips that are created.

Above One reason for using a video-editing program is to remove the corrupt frames that can often be found at the beginning and end of analog video sequences such as this. It's a simple job to trim them off.

Above-right Having split the sequence into separate chunks, you now have the ability to discard those bits that are obviously no good—out-of-focus shots, badly exposed clips, and so on.

Much of the footage fed into your computer or even copied directly to your standalone DVD recorder will be in a raw, unedited form and it could be that you want to perform a simple tidying-up job as you commit your analog assets to a digital future. It's a fact that the majority of home camcorder owners would like to undertake a degree of simple video editing merely to cut out the unwanted bits—such as false starts, accidental recordings and out-of-focus or defective footage. The good news is that this can be achieved with most modern computers and without any sophisticated applications or technology.

Cutting out the bad bits

This is an obvious first step on the road to creating perfect digital copies of your home-movie footage once it's in the digital environment. The important thing to remember is that as you cut, copy, and paste clips in your chosen computer editing program you won't incur any quality loss. Having converted analog recordings to the sequences of highly-complex binary numbers they now are, everything you do to your recordings will leave them in the same condition as they were when they first went digital. In digital form, it's easy to trim, cut, and copy clips and add them to others without fear of losing quality—in exactly the same way that you can scan a photograph and manipulate it in the ways explored in Section One.

All home cine and video footage has parts that could do with chopping out and tidying up. It could be that the cine film came to a roll-end at that point, or there might have been a slight problem with the film itself—such as over-exposure or light flare. Footage taken with earlier analog camcorders might suffer from awkward "clunky" edit points where the VHS, Video8, or Betamax tape was stopped and started. These things would be very difficult to sort out in their original formats, but thanks to the digital video-editing packages now available, it's very easy indeed.

Changing the order of clips on the timeline

Even the basic video-editing application that came on a disk with your camcorder will allow you to trim the beginnings and ends of clips in addition to enabling you to move them around on the timeline. Some applications—Microsoft Movie Maker and Apple iMovie being just two—give you the power to grab the "head" or "tail" of a clip and make the clip shorter or longer. The alternative, of course, is to literally chop off what you think you don't need—although you'll have to reload the clip into the timeline if you change your mind. Having decided on the preferred length of a number of clips on the timeline, you might also decide that clip 4 should be where clip 2 is—that's easy to do, and its a feature of every single editing program out there.

Left Drag a selected clip icon from iMovie's *Clips* pane and drop it into the desired position on the timeline, where it's immediately playable. This drag-and-drop capability is a feature of all mainstream digital video editing programs, and makes it very easy to build up sequences quickly.

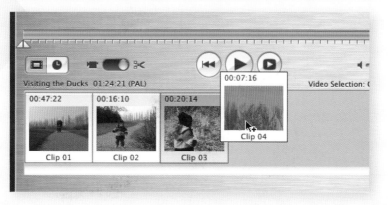

Right Having dropped a clip onto the timeline you may decide that it's better suited to another position. In this case, simply click and drag it to a new location. If you don't want to use it at all, then hit the Delete key—or place it back onto the *Clips* pane.

re-editing material continued

Crafting your footage

Whether your movie footage has been acquired from old analog video sources or by transferring cine film to video, the process of editing and reconstructing your footage is identical, regardless of the computer software being used. What's more, it's where you start to take control of your footage in a manner that's intended to entertain and enthrall your audience. In the main, of course, the primary reason for digitizing your movie assets is to apply a level of future-proofing to them; there will be a time in the not-too-distant future when you won't have ready access to a VHS, Betamax, or Video8 tape player—let alone an 8mm or 16mm film projector—so archive them now while you have the chance.

It's at the digital-editing stage that you find you suddenly have a marvellous opportunity to shape your raw material into a form that suits you, perhaps for the first time. Suddenly—and for very little financial outlay—you're able to not only cut out all the bits you don't want, but you can actively and creatively make a movie that you can be proud of.

Having selected clips one by one and trimmed them down to exclude all the embarrassing bits and segments that hadn't intended to be recorded, you're now in an ideal position to really build a new piece of work.

Piecing together the building blocks

With every shot you're telling a story that, in turn, builds into a sequence that carries depth and meaning for the viewer. If that sounds a bit high-brow, consider your view of many other home movies you've seen—do they engage you, or do they bore you after a few minutes? Although you're not always aware of it, almost everything you see on TV and in the cinema is edited with the object of carrying you along in a particular direction. Every shot in every sequence counts. And so it should be with your projects—even a simple re-edit of the contents of a load of 8mm cine-film canisters can be honed into shape. You may have lots of footage of the kids on the beach or granny taking the dog for a walk—but do you want every second of every shot? In fact, do you need every shot? Unless you have very particular reasons for keeping it, make every shot justify its existence and, if it serves no useful purpose, cut it out!

Looking for continuity

When piecing together clips of footage—however old and scratchy they are—consider assembling them in a sequence that conveys a sense of continuity. So,

Below Video clips are captured into the computer in the order that they appear on the tape, and your clips will be listed in the clip bin accordingly. If you wish, a whole range of the clips can be dropped onto the timeline at the beginning of your storytelling process.

Below The clips don't have to remain in their default order when added to the timeline. This is the perfect opportunity to reorganise the clips according to the story you want to tell. The clips can also be given more identifiable names.

Even though each of the shots in this example footage taken on a week away in the countryside is of a pastoral scene, the mood of the piece depends upon how each clip fits with those either side of it, so they combine to build a story.

if you have several rolls of footage taken on a particular vacation, make sure that you not only copy them in a chronological order, but that you also edit them in such a way that the viewer can gain a sense of time and place. If they're compiled out of sequence they won't mean much to anyone other than yourself—and in years to come that might cause a confusing problem for future generations!

So, if your week-long vacation involves a car journey, a ferry crossing, and a stay in a country cottage by the sea, make sure that the order in which they're transferred and edited reflects this. That's what's meant by the term "continuity." Get it wrong and your audience will become disorientated.

improving picture quality

Below Pinnacle's hugely popular, low-cost editing and DVD-creation program, called Studio, has a wide range of features designed to enable you to improve the visual properties of a clip. Here, you can make manual adjustments to the picture's RGB components.

The problem with older analog video and cine footage is that although the picture and audio quality seemed good at the time it was shot, much of your material will appear to be over-saturated with color, slightly contrasty, and perhaps even grainy. However, all is not lost; all beginner-level computer video-editing programs have some means by which your footage can be tidied up and brought back to life. You don't have to dig that far down into the menu system to see what utilities are offered to help you modify the color balance, brightness, and contrast.

With footage that was shot using older analog camcorders—especially those that employed color pickup tubes rather than CCDs and recorded to VHS and Betamax tape—you'll notice a tendency for the pictures to have a red bias if they were shot under artificial or low light. It's even more noticeable if a person is wearing a red shirt or jacket. The color will saturate—producing an image that's streaky and ill-defined. Unfortunately, you'll never be able to eliminate this completely, because this is what was recorded onto the tape, but features such as a color corrector will help you to redress the balance somewhat.

Adjusting the red, green, and blue picture elements

A television picture is made up of the three primary colors, namely red, green, and blue (or "RGB"). With red being the busiest, or highest-frequency, color on the light spectrum, it's the one that's most likely to break up at the recording stage. Too much red looks horrible on VHS and even Video8, but it can be reduced in applications such as Pinnacle's Studio editor, which offers a set of video filter tools that can be applied either to a single clip or to a whole sequence. As with many other programs, the selected filter (or

Left The horizontal green line that runs across the top of the clip in Pinnacle Studio 10 indicates that the computer is still rendering the transitions or effects applied to it. This is a common characteristic of many editing applications and the time taken to render is dependent upon the capabilities of your computer.

"video effect" in this case) is dropped onto the clip, after which manual adjustments can be made. The R, G, and B elements of the picture can be manually adjusted using the built-in slider controls and checked on the program's preview screen. Other programs offer a similar utility.

Using the same principle, it's possible to make your images brighter or darker in addition to having control over contrast.

Rendering

One thing you'll notice is that you will probably have to wait while your PC or Mac does a "catch-up" exercise after you've applied a filter to a clip or range of clips. This is called "rendering," and involves the program knitting together the filter effect and the clip to which it's applied. Although you're rarely aware of it, the program actually prepares a composite of all the elements in the form of a new temporary clip called a "render file." This is stored out of sight on the hard disk and is called up

by the program whenever you ask it to play back the sequence. The speed at which the program can perform this render varies considerably depending upon your computer's specification and the program itself. Once complete, the rendered sequence or clip can be played back smoothly, such as when editing with Apple's iMovie program. If a clip's properties are changed, however, a re-render will need to take place before the file is again complete and ready for playback.

Some higher-end PC and Apple Mac computer systems are powerful enough to offer what's known as "real-time" rendering and preview, meaning that you don't have to wait for this to happen—it's all performed in the background.

Above-left
Sometimes you may want to change a characteristics of a clip's color for creative effect. This is easily achieved and the results can be quite dramatic.

Above Microsoft's Movie Maker program identifies a clip to which a correction filter has been applied with a blue star. Here, you can see that the end point of the clip is being trimmed inward, an action that will require re-rendering of the clip. Movie Maker undertakes this task automatically.

applying transitions between clips

In contrast to a straight cut, which is an instantaneous change from the end of one clip to the beginning of the next, a transition makes the change between the clips gradually. The most common transition is a dissolve, or mix, in which the outgoing clip fades out at exactly the same rate as the incoming clip fades in. This overlap, or cross-fade, is used to move the viewer from one place and time to another. It's also used when you want to set up a slow, relaxed mood in your edited sequence. Other transitions include wipes in a wide range of shapes and two- and three-dimensional visual changes from one clip to another.

Applying a transition between clips

Imagine you've come to the end of a sequence in your movie and you want to transport the viewer to another time and place—perhaps you've just featured clips of the kids playing at home and now you want to move things on to the footage you took on a family vacation. A straight cut would suffice, but a dissolve (also called a cross-dissolve in some editing programs) makes for much more agreeable transition from one location to another.

All programs will have an easy way to select a transition, usually a pane or window within the main screen in which a range of thumbnail icons are displayed. It's quite possible that you'll be able to test the transition by clicking on it in order to obtain a preview in the main video window. Sometimes this will consist of a simple A/B graphic representing the "before" and "after" shots, while in other cases it will be possible to display the actual video clips. To preview, you must first apply the transition.

Drag your chosen transition icon down and drop it between the two video clips to which it is to be applied. Now you can easily preview it. You don't like it? Drop another one on top in substitution.

You'll also be able to vary the time that the transition takes; in some cases, extending or shortening its duration is as easy as dragging it left or right, whereas other programs give you the chance to enter a value using the keyboard. Remember that the duration of the transition will be measured in seconds and frames—with 25 frames per second being appropriate to PAL users, and 30 frames per second for NTSC. With two seconds often being the default transition, you probably won't have to change anything. A longer transition appears slow and lazy, it works well if accompanied by a suitable piece of music.

When to avoid transitions

It's important to offer a word of caution where transitions are concerned. In trying to persuade you to buy their editing software, many companies will proclaim their software offers a huge number of transitions, but don't be swayed. Their over-use can make your home movie project look cheap and tiresome to view, so apply them only when they're really needed. Watch a mainstream cinema movie and observe how many transitions you see—and apply the same professional standards to your project. You won't regret it.

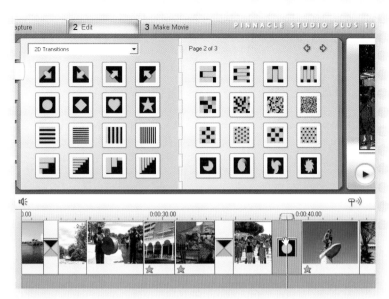

Left Pinnacle's Studio series of editing applications provide a wide range of basic transitions that can be applied to clips in either *Timeline* or *Storyboard* modes.

The transitions are represented by the black and green icons in the *Transitions* palette and also between clips on the timeline itself.

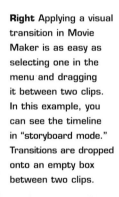

Right Applying a visual transition in Movie Maker is as easy as selecting one in the menu and dragging it between two clips. In this example, you can see the timeline in "storyboard mode." Transitions are dropped onto an empty box between two clips.

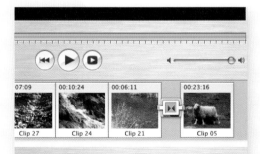

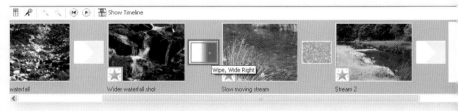

Above Although the screen appearance is different, the technique for applying a visual transition between clips is the same. Depending on your hardware, a short time will elapse (depicted by the red progress bar under the icon) while the transition is rendered.

Above In order to maintain the mood and feel of this sequence, we're applying a soft wipe transition. This produces a soft vertical wipe from left to right, revealing the second shot as it travels across the frame. Such transitions are good for depicting the passing of time.

applying transitions between clips continued

Using Storyboard and Timeline modes

You'll notice that the timeline that runs across the bottom of your video editor often provides two viewing modes. In all the main low-cost or freely bundled editing applications, there's a choice of "timeline" or "storyboard" modes. Again, the differences are superficial, and related only to variations in the user interface; the functionality is identical to the point where you should be able to switch from one application to another without needing to drastically re-learn techniques.

The storyboard mode is a simplified method of displaying clips, because they are assembled from left to right with any transitions placed visibly between the clips. This mode is ideal for complete newcomers to the art of digital video editing since the display offers a simple "building blocks" approach to the construction of a movie project. Switching to the alternative "timeline" mode is something that can be done at any time during editing and gives a more detailed view of the content of the timeline. If you feel the need to inspect the soundtrack in more detail prior to making specific adjustments, or you wish to add additional elements such as music or titles to your movie, then the "timeline" mode will be more appropriate. You can work in either mode at any time, switching between one and the other as the need arises.

What transition?

It's important to choose a transition that's appropriate for the context—and the content. If you're editing a nice, laid-back sequence containing gentle pastoral shots to be accompanied by a suitable piece of music, there's little point in placing eye-catching 3D transitions between shots where a simple dissolve will be more appropriate. A transition has to be right for the material and the mood you're trying to convey. The same goes for seemingly innocent transitions such as wipes; these are the sort of transitions in which a shape—perhaps a circle, square or multiple geometric shape—will effect the change from shot A to shot B. It could provide more of a distraction and bring no visual benefit at all, so if in doubt leave it out.

There could be situations where a particular transition—such as a circular wipe—could be appropriate when wiping from a shot of someone's eye to a different

Right The dissolve, or cross-fade from one clip to another, is the most basic transition, and one we see every day on TV and in films. It's very easy to apply and is probably one of the most effective.

Right Is a transition that consists of multiple circle wipes from one shot to another the most appropriate transition to be applied within a gentle pastoral sequence? Probably not. Consider the subject of the clips before choosing a transition to apply.

shot altogether. More complex transitions, such as page-turns, can be very effective when conveying a "going back in time" message in a visual sense. There are lots of transitions, both simple and highly complex, at your disposal in virtually all editing applications, all waiting to be explored. The joy of digital video editing is that you can try out any number at will until you find the one that works.

The benefits of using transitions

Transitions can greatly enhance your home movie project—both in terms of what you aim to achieve and also in the eyes of those family members and friends who'll be watching it. Most people only show their raw video footage to others, but a lovingly-constructed video sequence will make your project look professional by comparison—and you'll quickly attract praise as a result!

Above-right Movie Maker's screen layout has three main areas—the clip bin, preview window, and timeline. The layout may be unique to the application, but the principle is the same across all applications.

Right Transitions can be dropped into the little blue boxes situated between each clip in Movie Maker's storyboard view.

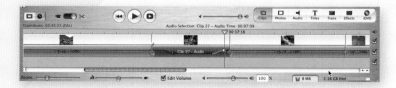

Left Switching from storyboard to timeline view in iMovie shows more detail of the content of the clips, the soundtracks, and of the settings found within each.

digital effects and filters

All digital video-editing programs offer a collection of effects and filters that can be used either to improve the appearance or sound of a clip or to spice up your moving images and sounds. Although the actual offering will vary from package to package, you'll usually find it possible to modify basic picture elements, such as brightness, contrast, and color balance in addition to changing the quality of recorded sound, adding echo, and so on.

apply a *Brightness & Contrast* adjustment filter to the clip, making the adjustments manually. Some applications will provide you with a real-time indication of the changes as you make them, while others will require a quick temporary render (this entails the program making a temporary reference file that is stored alongside your project files on the hard disk). Not only is it possible to combine one effect with another— brightness adjustments combined with color changes in addition to slow-motion effects, for instance—but it's also possible to undo applied effects and filters in almost all cases. So, if you decide that you don't like the effect, or effects that have been applied, you can simply revert to a clip's previous state.

Applying an effect or filter

In almost all cases, a video effect or filter is applied simply by selecting the effect in the menu and, after previewing if desired, dragging it to the timeline and dropping it on top of the clip or clips to which it is to be applied. If, for instance, your source footage is a bit dark, it's a simple job to

Correcting errors in old footage

Video effects and filters can also have a positive role to play in the restoration of old cine film and video footage. For example, take a piece of 8mm cine film that was shot and projected at either 16fps or 18fps (frames per second) that flickers heavily when being scanned by a video camera running at either 25fps (PAL) or 30fps (NTSC). You'll find that although the flicker will be barely noticeable to the human eye when playing the film on the projector, it will be considerably more evident when viewed on video. That's the result of an incompatibility between scanning rates; in short, they're not synchronous. While you can't eradicate this effect entirely, you can alleviate it either by using an electronic shutter built in to the camcorder (in the event that it has such a utility) or by using strobe filters in a video-editing program. This filter isn't available in all entry-level applications, but where it is, simply drag it to the timeline and make the appropriate adjustments for your clip.

Using motion effects

Speeding up or slowing down a clip is usually achieved by applying the appropriate filter from the menu. Many programs give you variable control over the speed adjustment, making it possible to see the results almost immediately. Apart from the positive impact of a slow-motion effect in sports sequences, for example, it can also make everyday shots look good—especially when assembled as part of a montage.

Above Pinnacle Studio's *Add Video Effect* menu contains a range of filters designed to help you improve and modify the appearance of your clips. In this instance, a *Noise Reduction* effect is applied to a clip containing grainy film footage.

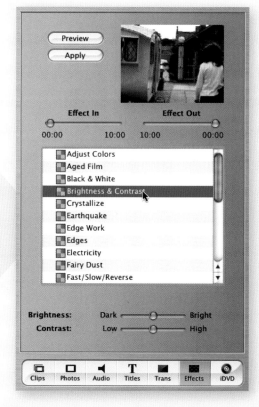

Right When you apply a filter to a selected clip in Apple's iMovie it's possible to obtain a moving-image preview. You can set the points at which the effect will start and stop within a clip, and to have manual control over its parameters—seen in the lower section of the window.

Above Varying the brightness of a clip in Studio is as simple as selecting the particular effect and then making a slider adjustment until you're happy with the results.

Note that it's also possible to enter a numeric value—useful in instances where you need to repeat the use of this setting across multiple clips.

improving and balancing sound

Without sound, you're left with a silent movie, and even if you've been digitizing old silent movies it's very likely that you'll be inspired to add either music, sound effects, or commentary (or a combination of all three) to your sequences at the editing stage. This is entirely possible; not only can you add music from your favorite CD (if you have permission, of course), but you can draw upon a program's built-in utilities to add sound effects and even so-called "instant music" loops and phrases to add spice to your project and provoke a favorable reaction from family members and friends. If your vacation movie or expedition video requires explanation, then write, record, and mix in your own commentary! Professional results are surprisingly easy with today's software, as you'll discover almost as soon as you start to explore the possibilities.

Above Apple's iMovie offers access to an impressive range of sound effects that are instantly available and that can be applied to the timeline in any combination and be modified at will. Here, you can see how the synch source sound levels have been modified, but how sound effects have also been added to a spare audio track underneath them.

Above The graphic equalizer in Pinnacle Studio makes it possible to filter or expand sounds within selected clips.

Above-right The audio tracks sit below the video track on almost all video editing program interfaces, as you can see here. Note the similarity between Pinnacle Studio's layout and others.

Synchronous pictures and sound

When you capture your footage from digital tape, or import video clip files from DVD, HDD (Hard Disk Drive), or SD card cameras, you'll also transfer the sound tracks that accompany the pictures automatically. That's because the two are embedded into the video stream. Once the clips appear in your clip bin and are available for inclusion in the edited project, the mere action of dragging each one to the timeline will result in both elements being added in combination. Most programs keep the video (the pictures) and the two parts of the stereo sound track locked together unless you tell the program otherwise. It also makes it easy to modify the sound levels—perhaps by changing the characteristics of the sound by applying limiters, increasing its overall level, adding echo, or adding filters that will help to reduce background noise such as hiss, and so on.

Not only can you manage the audible characteristic of an individual clip (or group of clips in combination), but you'll be able to "bend" and reshape the visible audio waveform in order to increase and decrease its intensity. This technique is often called "rubber-banding."

Adding audio tracks to the timeline

Look at any popular video-editing program and you'll see that you're given the opportunity to manipulate the content of more than one pair of stereo sound sources. The main source is, of course, the one that is associated with the camcorder footage itself (called the "synch sound source"), but extra tracks will be available for the addition of music, commentary, and sound effects according to the application in use. Each of these tracks can be used to build up a complex and professional-sounding audio track that will enhance your movie project no end—and will certainly impress your viewers! Sound is vital to a video production, as a viewing of any mainstream movie, TV show, or even commercial will tell you. Take away the sound and you're not left with much at all.

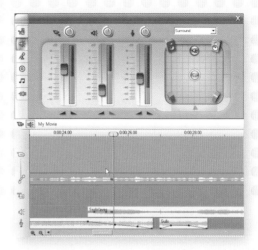

Left With the increasing use of 5.1 surround-sound systems in the home, Pinnacle's Studio provides a 5-channel surround-sound mixing panel that makes it possible to not only position sounds in the "3D-image" but also to pan it around in real-time.

Above SmartSound is a great utility for the creation of instant music accompaniment for your home video productions, and it provides a range of instrumentation loops in a wide variety of styles that can be applied to sequences with a mouse click.

Above Microsoft's Movie Maker conforms to the standard layout in which multiple sound-tracks run across the bottom of the screen within the timeline.

saving back to tape in the camcorder

Having copied your analog video footage into the digital domain, it's always a good idea to keep a master copy of sequences that have been polished and edited in the computer. This can be achieved in two ways. To start with, you could simply copy the finished projects from the computer back to the tape in the camcorder using the same connection you used to capture it in the first place—FireWire.

Making use of DV inputs

Outside Europe, almost all DV and Digital8 camcorders possess a two-way FireWire socket designed not only to provide a digital video output but also to accept incoming signals for re-recording to tape in the camcorder. This so-called "DV-in" utility (that can also now be found on an increasing number of European models) is very useful because it means that you can archive edited projects back to tape with no perceptible loss in visual or sound quality. Having archived your edited project masters back to digital tape, it's very convenient to place the tape back onto the shelf, clear the computer's hard disk of all the many project files, and get on with the next job. At any future stage you can then re-import the edited project (rather than the original tapes) with no quality loss and compile a DVD or export to a Web- or e-mail-ready format as is suited to your needs.

In order to make use of this handy feature, your camcorder must be equipped with a DV input capability, so check your user manual first. Alternatively, if you haven't yet purchased a camcorder, it's something that you might consider asking your retailer about.

What if my camcorder isn't a DV model?

FireWire is a standard feature of digital tape-based camcorders, such as MiniDV (or one of the professional-quality formats based on DV, like DVCAM or HDV) and Digital8, that record a DV-standard signal to Video8 and Hi8mm videocassettes. If you use a DVD camcorder, HDD (Hard Disk Drive), or SD card camera, you won't necessarily need to save back to the camcorder at all. The files they produce are smaller than those captured from DV and are consistent with DVD disk recordings in that they are saved using the same MPEG2 compression system. In such cases, all you need to do is to retain the edited project on disk as usual. Some people actually purchase a separate hard disk drive for the purpose of archiving their finished projects where they can all be accessed in one place.

Letting the software do the work

All applications that can capture and edit DV and Digital8 tape footage will allow you to re-record the finished project back to tape in the camcorder using DV-in. It's something that's as easy to achieve as it was to transfer it from the device in the first place. Where confusion can arise is in the fact that the camcorder should be placed in the "Play" or "VCR" mode; this will usually result in the camcorder displaying "DV in" in the viewfinder or LCD, letting you know that it's capable of accepting an external recording. Having done so, insert a blank cassette (it's probably a good idea to retain your original recordings) and follow the "Export to Tape" prompts in your editing program.

Above Premiere Elements is aimed at home users, but it has many of the features of its professional big brother program, Premiere Pro. Its export options are generous, with *Export to Tape* being just one that's available.

Right Microsoft's Movie Maker is an entry-level program that has a simple-to-use interface for exporting to a camcorder. It first has to create a render file of the project timeline that—for a moderate length movie—takes a few minutes.

Above Apple's iMovie is known for its simplicity. Here, the basic *Share* panel provides access to the whole range of export options, including the means to export your project back to digital tape in the camcorder.

adding DVD chapters and menus

Above The yellow diamonds that sit along the upper edge of the iMovie timeline show the chapter markers—the points users can jump to when playing the DVD.

Below After selecting a DVD screen template in Pinnacle's Studio application, it's then easy to set chapter points, indicated by a pink numbered flag, on the project timeline.

In order to produce DVD copies of your completed digital-video project files, it's necessary to prepare the edited sequences in a number of ways. During the process of capturing your clips from digital tape, your Windows PC or Apple Mac computer will have placed the clips into what's called a "wrapper format"—in the case of Windows this will result in an AVI file, whereas on a Mac it will be a MOV (basically QuickTime). Although they are stored in this format during the editing process, they will need to be converted to another format compatible with DVD players before starting the process known as "burning" the disk. Before that, however, you first need to split the contents of the timeline up into Chapters.

Setting chapter marks

A chapter mark identifies the point at which the player will arrive when you press the *Next* button on the DVD remote control, or when you ask to display the menu on the screen. Each discrete segment of the disk is called a chapter, so these need to be defined first.

Some programs, such as Pinnacle Studio and Apple iMovie (coupled with iDVD), make this process very easy. Other more sophisticated applications, such as Adobe Premiere Elements, also have built-in menu templates that make it very easy for you to choose the design and layout that best represents your subject matter (such as "Our Vacation," "Wedding," "New Baby," and so on) and then modify it to your own requirements. It's a good idea to experiment with the templates that are provided with all the main entry-level packages as a way of discovering for yourself what the possibilities are. Having done so, you'll then learn how they can be modified to your specific requirements—and it's also possible that you'll soon be creating your own from scratch.

Naming chapter marks

The creation of the markers that identify the beginning of a new chapter on the project timeline is as simple as clicking a menu option and setting the point according to either a timecode reference or the position of the timeline cursor or scrubber. In general, the setting of a chapter marker will result in a new menu

item being created that, in turn, might also produce a thumbnail image that can be selected by the user when wishing to jump to a particular sequence on the DVD playback. Some programs, such as Pinnacle Studio, are able to produce what's called a "motion menu thumbnail," in which the thumbnail itself comprises a short, cyclical video clip. Give careful consideration to how you name your markers because it's this that will appear on the screen—and long names won't always fit with your chosen design—they could even be truncated. Create short, simple names that identify what's in the sequence, and try not to create a large number of markers or you'll produce too many menu pages for your intended users to get through.

Using Easy DVD creation tools

Several of the consumer-level editing and DVD authoring packages now offer an instant means of creating a DVD from your edited sequences, and these are ideal if you're concerned about getting it right the first time. Basically, such programs will enable you to connect your DV or Digital8 camcorder to your computer via FireWire, after which the program will then rewind the tape, import your video footage and burn it direct to DVD. Chapter marks are usually generated at regular intervals, such as every five minutes.

Above It's very important to test the functionality of DVD menus prior to burning the final project to disk. Both Pinnacle Studio and Adobe Premiere Elements offer a preview screen designed to let you simulate all functions first, and it's here where any problems can be fixed prior to writing the disk.

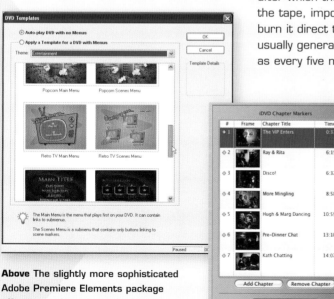

Above The slightly more sophisticated Adobe Premiere Elements package offers a number of standard menu templates that can easily be adapted for your own projects.

Left Having set the appropriate chapter marks, iMovie then gives you a list that can be edited before exporting the whole project to its sister application—iDVD, that is included with all new Apple Mac computers.

burning a DVD

After editing your home video project and setting out your chapter marks and menu settings, it's time to consider the creation of the disk itself. The process of undertaking all the preparatory work is called "authoring," with the process of actually writing all the information to disk being referred to as "burning."

The final thing that you need to consider is how the file will be converted from your computer to something that's readable by all standard DVD players. The common video standard for domestic DVD video playback is called MPEG2, which is a heavily compressed file that has to be made from your original edited AVI (Windows) or MOV (Mac) project files. In almost all cases, this conversion process is virtually invisible—the wizards that you're asked to follow in the starter programs make it very easy for you to create DVD-ready files from your sequences, and you don't have to worry at all. However, it's worth bearing in mind that a single-sided DVD disk will allow you up to 4.7GB of disk space (or 8GB for dual-layer disks), so there's obviously a limit to the amount of video you can put onto a disk.

Disk formats

In addition to the DVD-R/+R (recordable once-only) and DVD-RW/+RW rewritable disk formats, there are other options you may want to consider when archiving and sharing your digital video project. For projects lasting 30 minutes or less, you may wish to save your project to S-VCD rather than DVD. It uses the same MPEG2 compression format as DVD, but plays tricks with the vertical resolution of the picture by reducing the effective number of pixels and stretching the picture on playback. For good, steady material that doesn't contain a lot of extraneous movement this can be an adequate and low-cost substitute that facilitates the use of cheaper CD-R and CD-RW disks rather than the slightly more expensive DVD alternatives. Almost all common Windows-based disk-authoring applications will provide this alternative to DVD, in addition to the more heavily compressed and lesser-quality VCD variant that uses MPEG1 instead of MPEG2.

Bit rates and volume

Unlike the captured digital video file formats DV-AVI and DV-MOV (Windows and Apple Mac respectively), that have a fixed compression system and data rate, MPEG2 can be varied according to the space on the disk available and the overall content of the edited video itself. In general, home DVD players can support a bit-rate—that is, the rate at which the stream of data can be moved efficiently from one place to another within a digital system—in excess of 7,000kbps (thousand bits per second), and at 6,000kbps it's possible to store up to 120 minutes of good-quality video onto a standard single-sided DVD disk (with a capacity of 4.7GB). Should you wish to squeeze more onto a disk, it will be necessary to use a lower bit-rate, resulting in a greater compression of the data and potentially more noticeable "artifacts" on playback. In general, the higher the bit-rate, the better the visual and aural quality. 6,000kbps is generally acceptable, but your authoring program should sort this out for you by matching the disk capacity with the duration of your project.

Creating DVDs the quick and easy way

With the low cost of standalone domestic DVD recorders, it's possible that you may want to use this as the means to produce your DVD disks rather than take the computer-based authoring route. With several models of recorder now offering FireWire input sockets, it's even possible to transfer the sequences that have been edited and copied to DV or Digital8 tape in your camcorder direct to DVD disk. The downside is that the recorder might not add chapter markers that are specific to each discrete section.

Above Aimed more at the enthusiast, but still accessible to beginners, Premiere Elements features a straightforward workflow design for authoring a DVD from the content on the timeline. As with other programs, Elements has a wide number of template menu styles and buttons to choose from. A finished DVD is only a few clicks away from this point in the process.

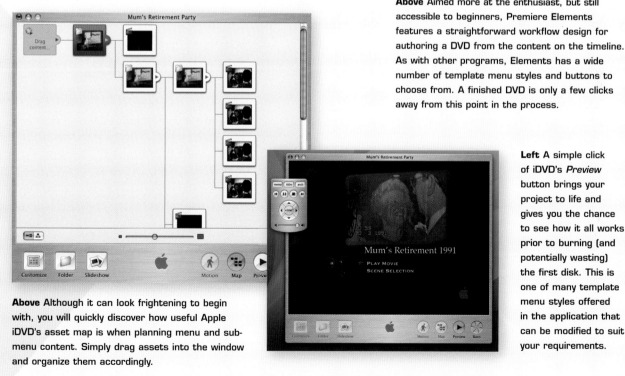

Above Although it can look frightening to begin with, you will quickly discover how useful Apple iDVD's asset map is when planning menu and sub-menu content. Simply drag assets into the window and organize them accordingly.

Left A simple click of iDVD's *Preview* button brings your project to life and gives you the chance to see how it all works prior to burning (and potentially wasting) the first disk. This is one of many template menu styles offered in the application that can be modified to suit your requirements.

exporting for the Web

Left Movie Maker provides a wide range of specific export options, including one for 512kbps broadband playback. This produces a file which is 320 x 240 pixels wide when viewed in Windows Media Player.

Left Using a codec (compression/ decompression) setting suited to ordinary 56kbps dial-up Internet, you're faced with a much smaller window size and a considerable reduction in sound and picture quality.

Left Along with the Web, you can also export video to a number of common portable devices.

It's increasingly likely that, in addition to authoring DVD versions of your edited video projects and copying back to tape in the camcorder, you'll want to configure your movie for sharing with friends and family members over the Internet. With the widespread use of broadband connections, many people are now realizing the benefits of being able to send and receive good quality video clips at a speed that simply wasn't possible on dial-up connections.

Also, more and more people are exchanging short video clips via their cell phones, PlayStation Portables, and iPod Video devices, so why not take full advantage of this exciting new range of distribution options?

Compressing for the Web

All popular video-editing and export programs contain utilities designed to enable the easy, hassle-free, conversion of your full-screen digital video files to those formats appropriate to sharing over limited bandwidth. Even though your broadband Internet connection might be fast, it still has its restrictions—and there's no way you'll be able to share your clips unless they're reduced in window size (the size at which they're viewed onscreen) and file size. That entails compression using similar techniques appropriate to DVD authoring— only with much greater compression rates.

In order to view video files over the Internet, the end user will need to use a software player. Common examples of these include Microsoft Windows Media Player, Apple QuickTime, and Real Networks' Real Player. Other choices include Macromedia Flash and DivX (although the latter is more suited to

Left Apple's iMovie HD offers a simple set of export choices, including a home page option that prepares your movie for uploading to its .Mac Web-hosting utility.

desktop computer and disk playback). By using the first two, you'll cover most of the user base, and there are versions for Windows PCs as well as Apple Mac.

Export Presets

All the programs featured in the previous pages will point you towards the use of presets according to the likely user bandwidth (the estimated Internet speed of those who will download your movies). At its simplest, this will be three settings—slow dial-up modem, medium-speed broadband (also referred to as DSL), and faster broadband. If a user is accessing the clip via a company network, this can be even higher. In many North American and Western European countries, it's reasonable to assume that most broadband users will have DSL (Digital Subscriber Line) connection speeds of at least 512kbps, so you may want to tailor your files accordingly. There's nothing to stop you from producing, and making available more than one version of your video, of course. Whether you create snail-speed dial-up modem versions is your choice, but with so many broadband users, few people bother these days.

Uploading your movie to a Web server

In order to make your movie available to others over the Internet, you'll need to place it onto a Web server. That isn't as complicated as it sounds; Microsoft, Apple, Pinnacle, and Ulead all offer free Web hosting services where your video clips, photos, and sounds can be saved—just sign up, follow the wizards at the end of the export process and you're almost done. In most cases, the system will even help you to send out an e-mail to your friends and family informing them of your latest offering and where it can be found.

Above More advanced settings are also available, such as a one-click export to your iPod Video, 3G cell phone, or PDA. As your experience and confidence grows, you'll want to make more use of the wide range of very specialized QuickTime export options.

section three
music

recording from vinyl

Above It's perfectly possible to transfer audio from your vinyl LPs into a digital format on your computer. The most important thing to bear in mind is that the sound will need to pass through a preamp unless the turntable has one built in.

Above Most audio devices use stereo RCA plugs for output, and these will need to be converted to a MiniJack plug in order to attach them to a computer.

Whether for the sake of perceived sound quality, authenticity, or nostalgia, many music lovers cherish their vinyl LPs. A little plastic CD case simply does not do justice to classic album cover art. Plus, there is a simple, satisfying beauty in the ritual of carefully placing a stylus on a spinning record in order to hear a favorite track.

Nevertheless, anyone who has tried to haul a cherished record collection into a new apartment or house knows just how unwieldy and brutally heavy the humble LP can become in numbers. And why is it that every shelf seems to be just a little smaller than twelve inches high? Even the most open-minded music collector will admit that at some stage it becomes unacceptable to have hundreds of records lined up on the floor along one wall of your den.

Even if you store them correctly, records do sustain a significant amount of wear with normal use. In fact, many audiophiles claim that you should never even play individual tracks on an album—the needle should be deposited carefully at the beginning and only removed from the surface at the end in order to minimize the possibility of scratching.

Recording your albums onto your computer allows you to listen to them repeatedly without wearing down the record surface. It also allows you to transfer all the songs on the album to a CD (see pages 100–103) or personal music player (see pages 104–105) if you wish. Virtually any all-in-one home computer package now comes equipped to perform these tasks right out of the box. Your sound card—the hardware component that converts analog audio to digital signals, and vice versa—will have a stereo Line In jack on the back of the computer case, and often a more convenient jack at the front of the box. This will also be the case on budget-priced, sound card-free computer models with audio hardware built-in.

This Line In jack will often be a small ⅛" stereo phono plug jack, also known as a MiniPlug jack, or a MiniJack. Most turntables connect via a cable with two RCA plugs for the left and right stereo channels, so you would need an RCA-to-⅛" adapter to plug the turntable into the sound card, but in most cases this will not work properly unless your turntable has a built-in preamplifier to bring the signal up to the correct level for recording (known as the line level). Many newer model turntables do offer built-in preamps, and inexpensive turntable preamps are available that serve the same purpose—these are often designed for use with computer sound cards.

If your turntable is plugged into the "Phono" (short for "phonograph," in this case) jacks on a stereo amplifier or receiver, it is perfectly acceptable to use an RCA-to-⅛" adapter from the Line Out or Tape Out jack on the back of the amp to connect to the Line In jack on any sound card. Note that the microphone input on your sound card is not designed for stereo signals, because it is usually a mono jack, and be careful—using other outputs to connect to your sound card may damage it. Higher-end sound cards will offer "breakout boxes," which are components the same size as a CD or DVD drive that fit into one of the drive bays. These offer various inputs on the front panel, usually including dual RCA jacks, often with turntable preamps.

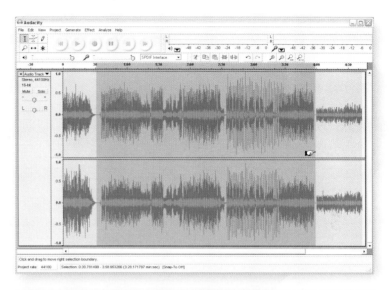

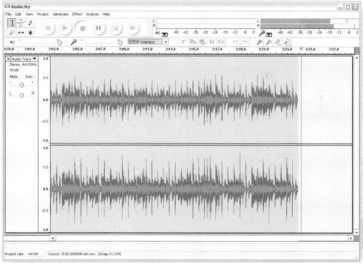

Above Most audio-editing programs will allow you to view your recording as "waveforms." These are essentially graphical representations of the track, with the time running along one axis, and the volume along the other. Loud parts of the track will have higher peaks than quiet parts. The two waveforms shown in the program Audacity above represent the left and right channels of the stereo sound.

recording from vinyl continued

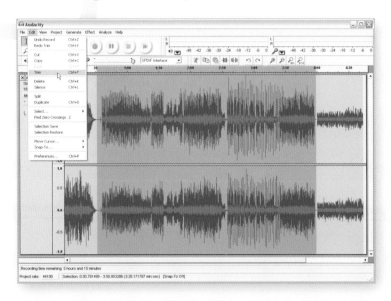

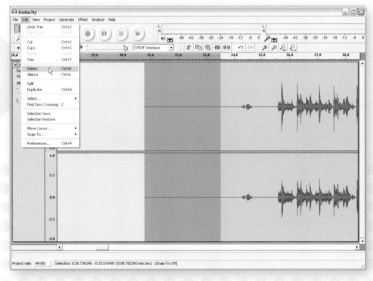

Top In audio software, the *Cut* command deletes the current selection, and the *Trim* command deletes everything except the selection.

Above It's a good idea to cut away excessive areas of silence (shown by a flat line in the waveform) at the beginning and end of your tracks.

The age of the stylus on your turntable will greatly affect the quality of the sound, not to mention the degree of wear your records will have to endure. It is worth making a trip to a high-end stereo component shop to replace that old cartridge if a new one is available. The quality of the cables you use is also a factor, and while you might not immediately notice the difference in sound quality between a cheap plastic RCA cable and a well-insulated one with gold-plated plugs, repeated listens to a digital music file will eventually reveal every single little flaw in your original recording. This can become annoying, so it is best to use the highest-quality accessories you can afford from the beginning.

Another consideration is electrical grounding. Most newer turntables are self-grounded, but many older models have a separate grounding wire that is meant to be attached to whatever device you're plugged into, such as an amplifier. Without grounding of any kind, an audible hum will pervade your recordings.

Both Windows and Macintosh operating systems are equipped to record audio. Sound Recorder is the default recording application on Windows machines, and GarageBand is the nearest equivalent on modern MacOS machines. Of course, there are many other audio software applications for both platforms, and many are free, so use the one you prefer.

Once you've found a way to plug your turntable into your computer, and have chosen your recording application, make sure that your software-based volume settings are set to allow input on the jack to which you have connected your turntable, such as Phono or, if you are using a preamp, Line In. You will need to set the levels so that the highest signal—the loudest sounds from the record—peak at just under 0dB (decibels). This will ensure that you get the highest possible signal with a minimum amount of hiss and external noise. Many software programs will monitor sound levels visually, warning you when the signal is near peak as well as when it has gone over peak levels, or "clipped." Unlike recording to a cassette, where volume saturation can be acceptable, any volume over an acceptable limit on a digital recording will produce clipping—this will be represented in the resulting digital file by audible distortion.

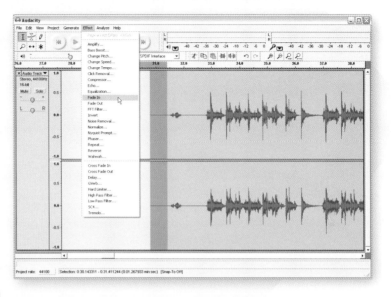

Above Stereo RCA plugs are the standard for connecting audio devices together.

Above Professional sound cards come with their own applications for changing settings.

This card even has an option for setting a "curve" filter to apply to your recording.

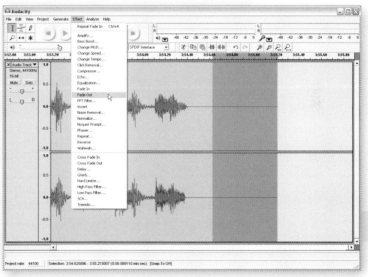

Above In addition to cutting silence from the beginning and end of your tracks, it's also a good idea to apply a short fade in at the start and fade out at the end. This helps to prevent any obvious digital clicks or pops that can appear when a sound is suddenly cut.

recording from vinyl continued

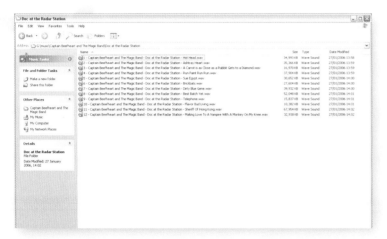

Above Make sure that you always give logical names to your recorded tracks on the computer, and you follow the same consistent rules with all of your tracks. Modern computers allow you to have long filenames, so don't feel like you need to compress everything down to a few characters.

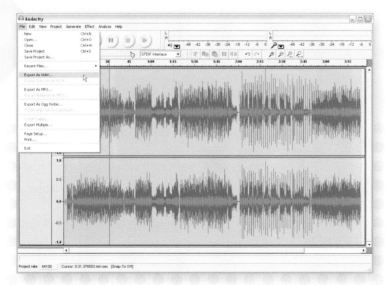

Above If you want to keep your recording at the optimal digital quality, make sure that you export it as a WAV file. Even if you later convert the file to a compressed MP3 for playback, it's worth keeping the WAV file as backup.

Your sound card will convert the analog sound to digital data, and the software will write this data to your hard drive. Your initial recording should be made in WAV format on a Windows machine or in AIFF format on a Macintosh (for more information on file formats see pages 90–91). Both formats are uncompressed and produce large files at CD-level quality: about 10 megabytes per minute of audio. CD-quality audio requires a bit depth of 16 and a sample rate of 44.1kHz (kilohertz), which is ideal for your recording. Many sound cards will allow you to record with higher bit depths and sample rates, but this is overkill for recording music from vinyl. It is best to start the recording just before you play the LP, and let it run for the entirety of each side of the album, because you can separate and trim the silences from individual tracks later. Some software packages can be configured to detect the gaps between songs—don't use this feature, as it will count in-song silences as track dividers, and in popular, jazz, or orchestral music these occur more frequently then you might imagine.

Don't do anything else with your computer while it is recording; don't even surf the Web or check your e-mail! Your system will be writing to the hard drive as quickly as it can, and any secondary activity could produce unwanted glitches in the file.

Once you have both sides of the album recorded and saved, you may want to clean up and normalize the tracks (see pages 92–97). Then, you will have to extract each individual song from the recorded files, preferably with a visual interface and a graphical representation of the recorded waveforms so that it is obvious where each track begins and ends.

There are many options, but for the sake of this example, we will use Audacity—a freely downloadable program with a simple visual interface for Windows and Mac.

Listen carefully to the beginning and end of the first song, watching to see where the true beginning and end are represented on the waveform. This is to ensure that you don't cut off a "fade-out" or other sonic element. Carefully select the first song, leaving some space at the beginning and end, then trim it using *Edit > Trim*.

Select a small amount at the beginning of the track and choose *View > Zoom to Selection*. Re-select and delete some of the silent portion off the beginning—how much silence you leave is up to you, but it is best to leave less than a second. Then, select yet another tiny amount right at the beginning and choose *Effect > Fade In*. This will eliminate any electronic "pops" or other sounds that sometimes occur when a digital audio file is trimmed. Once you are done editing the beginning of the track, zoom in to the end of the track and repeat the process, using *Fade Out* instead of *Fade In*.

The *Save* feature in most audio software saves the file in a proprietary format for editing later. To save the file in a playable format, you will need to *Export* it under the *File* menu. You can export to an uncompressed WAV or AIFF format if you want the best quality or if you intend to burn the tracks to CD (see pages 100–103), or you can save time at this stage by exporting directly to MP3 format for storage on your hard drive or transfer to your personal music player.

You will need to reopen the original WAV file you recorded and repeat this process to trim out each individual track. After this, you can delete the original

> ### VINYL CURVE FILTERS
>
> Due to the physical limitations of vinyl LPs, they are engraved with the bass levels reduced and the treble levels increased. Your turntable preamplifier applies a complex mathematical formula that compensates for this by boosting the bass levels and reducing the high-frequency noise created by the needle moving in the record groove during playback. The most common of these formulas is known as the RIAA curve, but there are many others. If you have old recordings, then you may need to apply these formulas in your software package after the file is imported in order for the track to play back correctly.

WAVs as you will still have your "master copy"—the vinyl record—available should you need to re-record it later.

While it will not be necessary to distinguish between tracks from Side A or Side B, you should name each digital file with the track number, the artist's name, the title of the album, and the track title, in that order. This will ensure that the tracks not only sort themselves in the correct order, but each track will also be instantly identifiable on its own. You should also have a folder for each artist, containing individual subfolders for each album, single or EP.

Once you have extracted and exported the tracks, you will be able to play them back as many times as you like. While there is not as much tactile interaction involved, you can be sure that every note of your original albums will remain intact.

Above Microsoft Windows comes with a basic audio-editing package called Sound Recorder that will enable you to make limited alterations to your WAV files.

recording from audio tape

Compact cassette tapes were designed to be portable, but not necessarily to be durable. As tape stock ages, it is susceptible to wear and breakage, particularly when the fast-forward and rewind functions are the only rapid means of accessing a particular song on an album.

No preamplification is required to connect a cassette deck to your computer. Simply connect an RCA cable to the Line Out or Tape Out jacks on the deck, and connect the other end of the RCA cable to the Line In jacks on your sound card. If the Line In jack is a ⅛" phono plug jack, use an RCA-to-⅛" plug adapter, as shown on page 80.

If your tape deck only offers a headphone jack as an output, you can use a cable with stereo ⅛" plugs at either end to connect it to your computer. Before you adjust the sound card input level, be sure to adjust the headphone volume on the tape deck to about two-thirds of full volume—too low a level will allow a great deal of background noise, and too high may introduce distortion. You may have to

experiment to find just the right volume, as this can vary.

The procedure for transferring taped audio to your computer is much the same as that for recording vinyl (see pages 80–85). There may be a tone at the beginning of Side A and at the end of Side B that can be trimmed out.

If the cassette was recorded using a specific type of Dolby noise reduction, this should be enabled on the tape deck before you record to your computer, unless it is Dolby HX Pro, which was designed to play back on any deck without having to be "decoded." If no noise reduction settings were used when the tape was recorded, then do not use the noise reduction settings on the deck. Audio software offers more powerful and flexible methods of reducing hiss and noise once the tracks are recorded to your hard drive. For example, Audacity software lets you select a portion of the recording with a noise or hiss that you want to eliminate throughout the track. Select some of the "silent" portion of your recording and choose *Effect > Noise Removal* from the top menu; then, click on *Get Noise Profile* in the dialog box that appears. Choose *Effect > Noise Removal* again, and you will be asked to what degree you wish to remove the noise that the software detected.

The above procedure can be used with your recorded vinyl as well. Be sure to listen to the result before saving the file—if it is unsatisfactory you can always *Undo* (Ctrl+Z on Windows; Cmd+Z on a Mac).

There is an easy way to tell the difference between a mono phono plug and a stereo phono plug. The stereo plug will have two stripes around the plug, while the mono has only one. This applies to both the ¼" and ⅛" (MiniPlug) varieties.

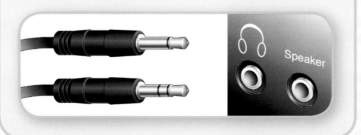

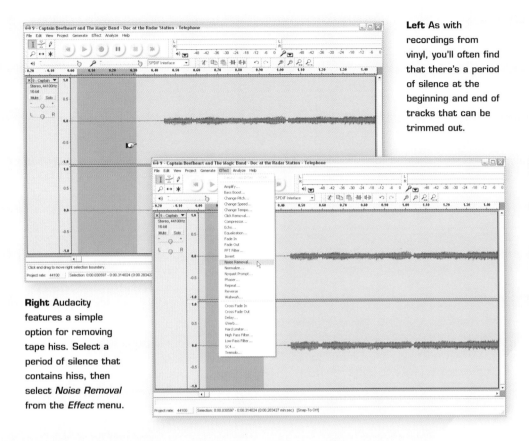

Left As with recordings from vinyl, you'll often find that there's a period of silence at the beginning and end of tracks that can be trimmed out.

Below Noise removal software analyzes noise on a part of the track that should be silent, and then uses that profile to remove similar nose from the rest of the track.

Right Audacity features a simple option for removing tape hiss. Select a period of silence that contains hiss, then select *Noise Removal* from the *Effect* menu.

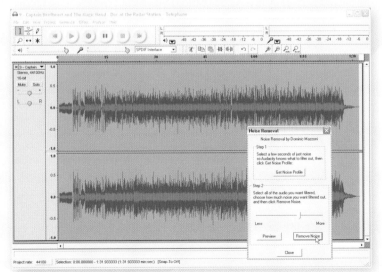

Left Once you have the profile of the noise—in this case, tape hiss—you can easily remove that noise from the remainder of the track.

WARNING!

In the rare instance that a set of RCA jacks are meant to go from your stereo into a set of unpowered speakers, do not plug these into your sound card. Similarly, never connect the speaker outputs from your amplifier to your sound card, as the high level of output will do a great deal of damage to the delicate electronics in your computer.

importing CDs and MiniDiscs

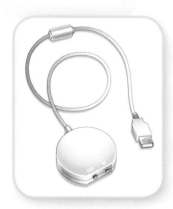

Above In the event that your computer does not offer an audio input, you may need to invest in a USB audio interface. There are inexpensive devices that will do the job, such as the Griffin Technology iMic 2, that offers line level and microphone level input, and a basic stereo output.

WARNING!

When applicable, don't forget to plug your devices into a wall socket when transferring audio to your computer—you don't want a dying battery to interfere with your recording!

Importing CDs

All modern computers are equipped with CD-ROM or DVD-ROM drives, and digital extraction—"ripping"—of audio should be possible using basic, free software, such as iTunes. Simply insert your CD in the drive, select it in the menu, and click the *Import CD* button in the top right corner of the iTunes interface. In most cases, this will encode the music from the CD into the default AAC or MP3 format.

On Macs you should not encounter any problems with this, but on a Windows machine, you may need to check your CD-ROM settings. To do this in Windows XP, right click on your CD or DVD player in the *Device Manager* and select *Properties* in the menu that appears. Then, click on the *Properties* tab in the dialog box that comes up, and make sure the checkbox beside *Enable digital CD audio for this CD-ROM* device is selected. If it is not selected by default, it could be that your drive is either not connected properly, or it simply does not support digital audio playback and extraction.

If you want to take more control over the ripping process, you can set the compression format in your music-management software (see pages 90–91 for more on compression formats). If you want to make a perfect digital copy of the music on the CD, then you should transfer it to your computer as a WAV or AIFF file.

Importing MiniDiscs

CDs store audio in an uncompressed (often called "lossless") format, and the files produced when transferring digitally from a CD to the hard drive should be identical to one another. MiniDiscs can also store audio

in a lossless digital format, but to get more time out of a MiniDisc, ATRAC (Adaptive Transform Acoustic Coding) compression is often used (see pages 90–91). Lower compression ratios produce imperceptible distortion, but higher levels produce audio artifacts that cannot be removed. Simply put, these files will not sound as good as uncompressed files, and no amount of manipulation is going to improve them.

The transfer of music from MiniDisc to your computer should be done digitally. Because the music is stored as digital information, using an audio cable—an analog connection—will require the device to convert the digital signal to an analog one to be sent to the computer; at this point it will have to be reconverted to a digital format. Not only will slight inaccuracies be introduced during the conversions, but distortion can be produced in the cable.

If you are going to invest in an external audio component it might be worth investing in a higher-quality unit that you can use with all of your devices, such as the M-Audio Mobilepre USB, which is powered from the USB port, offers digital input, and has a built-in preamp. Most of these components include a range of helpful digital audio software packages as well.

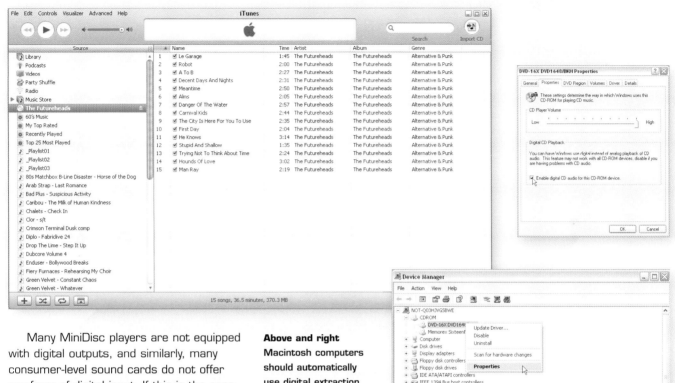

Many MiniDisc players are not equipped with digital outputs, and similarly, many consumer-level sound cards do not offer any form of digital input. If this is the case with your setup, you should obtain a high-quality cable to connect the Line Out or the headphone jack of your device to the Line In on your sound card, and record the audio in much the same manner that you would a cassette tape (see pages 86–87).

If your MiniDisc player supports digital output, then it will often include software enabling you to take advantage of this, but you must also have a digital input on your computer. This will take the form of either a coaxial input to be used with a coaxial cable, or an optical input that will either be a square or ⅛"-sized optical jack. Both plugs emit a red light when attached to a working device. Optical-to-coaxial adapters are available if necessary. Sony's Net MD allows digital transfers from computer to MiniDisc via USB, but not vice-versa.

Above and right Macintosh computers should automatically use digital extraction methods with built-in CD drives, so you shouldn't need to worry about them. On a PC, you may need to check that this option is enabled for optimum recording quality.

Right Optical connections will usually have plugs to fit into the sockets when they aren't in use to prevent dust interfering with the data transmission.

file formats

There are many proprietary file formats that are native to specific audio software, particularly in the field of audio production, but the following list covers the most common music file formats and codecs (compressor/decompressors) used by most computer systems and audio software.

Typically compressed formats:

MP3: The revolution in digital audio has been led by one specific audio file format called MPEG Audio Layer 3, or MP3. Based on a series of international standards of audio and video compression called MPEG (Moving Picture Experts Group), MP3 is a file format that allows audio data to be digitally compressed to a chosen degree by compressing or simplifying parts of the music that are perceived less by the human ear. Generally speaking, the higher the compression, the lower the quality of the compressed audio; nevertheless, even at near-CD quality, using a bitrate of 128kbps (kilobits per second; that is using 128,000 bits of data to represent each second of music), MP3-encoded audio is about one-twelfth the size of ordinary uncompressed audio.

This is important, because it allows the transfer of high-quality audio data over networks or the Web in a fraction of the time it normally would; as such, MP3 files are currently the standard for the online broadcast of music. Plus, it allows for many more songs to be stored on a hard drive or memory chip.

This makes the sale of music on a downloadable, song-by-song basis possible and economically viable, and it allows personal music players to store a huge volume of digital audio. It also makes piracy of the type that used to happen with dual cassette decks much easier and more widespread, but fortunately, many record labels have reported increased sales as a result of giving away MP3 tracks on their websites. This could be due to the fact that word of mouth has increased interest and demand all over the world, but in any event, artists, distributors, and companies must continue to adapt. The technology is only going to get more powerful with the integration of Surround capability and other innovations (see page 104).

WMA or ASF: The Windows Media Audio format is Microsoft's competitor to MP3. It is often contained within an Advanced Systems File (ASF) if it includes other information as well as audio. The latest versions offer surround sound and digital rights management (anti-piracy) support.

AAC: Advanced Audio Coding is Apple's offering as a competitor to MP3 and is used by iTunes and QuickTime. These use the audio-based portions of MPEG-4 media standards—agreed upon by the Moving Picture Experts Group—and usually have an .M4A file extension.

OGG: OGG Vorbis is a patent-free format developed by the Xiph Open Source Community, part of a non-profit corporation "dedicated to protecting the foundations of Internet multimedia from control by private interests." The files are inherently variable-bitrate and can be encoded on a scale of quality from one to ten, with six being roughly CD-quality and three being the competitive equivalent to a 128kbps MP3.

Below Analog sounds contain continuous, smooth sound waves, enabling pure, high-fidelity audio. Digital sounds are made up of samples taken at set periods of time—for example, sound on a CD is sampled at 44,100 times per second. This is unnoticeable by the human ear, but decreasing the number of samples per second can lead to obvious glitches in the audio.

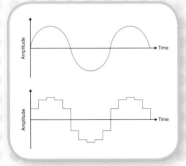

ATRAC: Adaptive Transform Acoustic Coding is a compression algorithm developed by Sony for use on MiniDiscs and other devices. May include OpenMG, a digital rights management scheme developed by Sony—these files will have .OMG or .OMA extensions.

RealAudio: A format designed by RealNetworks for streaming over the Internet, that uses various compression codecs and will have the file extension .RA, .RM, or .RAM.

AC-3: Adaptive Transform Coder 3—the codec commonly known as Dolby Digital—is a standard for audio on DVDs.

MP4: A "container" file format based on MPEG-4 audio and video standards, that can include various forms of media, including MP3-based audio.

Typically uncompressed formats:
WAV or WAVE: The Windows wave file is the generic audio format on Windows PCs, using Pulse Code Modulation (PCM) to represent the audio in basic binary—this is not unlike the way a generic text file is stored, as it is uncompressed and can be read by any computer. It can allow various sample sizes at various sample rates; CD-quality audio requires a sample rate of 44.1kHz and a sample size or bit depth of 16 bits, meaning that the audio is represented, or "captured," 44,100 times per second using samples of 16 bits at a time.

There are various compression schemes that can be used to reduce the size of WAV files, but these tend to reduce compatibility with some programs or systems, and they are not as effective as MP3.

Professional audio applications offer the ability to process (open and edit) or render (save) WAV files at higher sample rates and bit depths—popularly, 24-bit samples at 96kHz—but this requires a sound card that will support these files as well as a powerful computer.

AIFF or AIF: The Audio Interchange File Format was developed by Apple and is equivalent to Microsoft's WAV format, also using the PCM codec.

AU: The Sun Microsystems default format is equivalent to WAV or AIFF and readable on most platforms.

CDDA or CDA: The PCM-based format for CD audio is limited to a sample rate of 44.1kHz and a sample size of 16 bits.

PCM QUICK SPECS (WAV, AIFF, AU, CDDA)
Sample size range: usually 8, 16, or 24 bits

Sample rate range: typically 8 (telephone quality) to 192 (far beyond CD quality) kHz

Suggested sample size and rate: CD-quality audio demands 16-bit samples at 44.1kHz

Approximate file size per minute of stereo audio: About 10 megabytes

MP3 QUICK SPECS
Bitrate range: 8–320kbps

Sample size range: usually 44.1kHz

Suggested bitrate: 192kbps provides excellent, CD-quality audio with a good degree of compression. Variable bitrate encoding can reduce file size farther if your audio software allows it.

Approximate file size per minute of stereo audio: 1.4 megabytes at 192kbps, 1 megabyte at 128kbps (sample rate of 44.1kHz)

cleaning up recordings

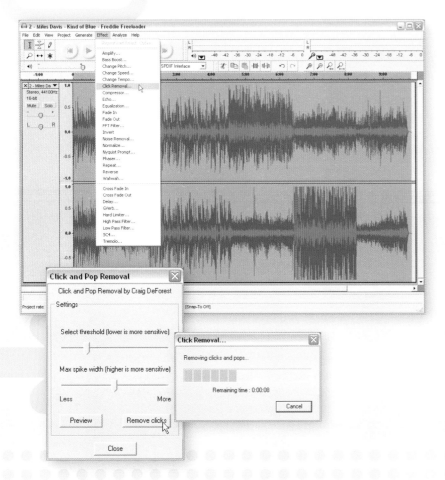

Above Audible clicks and pops are common problems with digital sounds, especially when they are highly compressed. Many audio-editing programs will come with features for removing this unwelcome noise.

No amount of digital processing and mouse clicking is ever going to fix a poorly recorded track. However, you can make many improvements to flawed recordings; in fact, there are a plethora of specialized software programs designed for these specific functions.

There is no reason to go out and spend loads of money on a batch of new software when the ability to clean up your recordings is available for free with a few minutes of Web searching, some research

and perhaps a little experimentation. The freely downloadable Audacity audio software is a good place to start.

See pages 86–87 for information on basic noise removal—particularly where the music is much louder than the noise, such as with tape hiss. Here, we will begin with more jarring audio anomalies, often referred to collectively as "clicks and pops." These can occur as a result of noise on a scratchy old LP you used as a source for a recording, or they can be digital glitches in a badly encoded audio file. Either way, the track will never sound pristine unless you can re-record it, but you may be able to make a subtle improvement if the original source is not available.

Open the track in Audacity with *File > Open*, then make sure you can see the entire waveform as clearly as possible by choosing *View > Fit in Window* and then *View > Fit Vertically*. This way, you'll be able to see the changes you make as clearly as possible.

Select the entire waveform by choosing *Edit > Select > All*, then choose *Effect > Click Removal*. The dialog box that appears will give you adjustable options, but the best option to start is to use the defaults. Press the *Remove Clicks* button.

Listen to the resulting track, then select *Edit > Undo* and listen to the original as a comparison. The clicks may be less apparent, but does the presence or volume of the music suffer as a result? You can *Redo* and *Undo* as many times as you like, or use the *Preview* setting on the *Click and Pop Removal* dialog box while adjusting the settings. At higher settings, the *Threshold* slider will remove less sound. The *Max Spike Width* slider refers to spikes in the

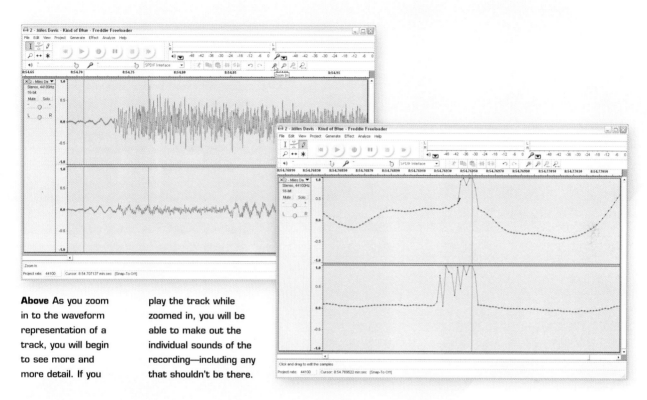

Above As you zoom in to the waveform representation of a track, you will begin to see more and more detail. If you play the track while zoomed in, you will be able to make out the individual sounds of the recording—including any that shouldn't be there.

Above Zooming all the way in with Audacity allows you to see each of the digital samples in the track. Clicks in the sound will show up as obvious spikes that, with a bit of practice, you should be able to "paint out" using the *Draw* tool.

waveform, because clicks tend to be very narrow spikes—a higher setting will thus remove a wider range of noises, but may interfere with actual musical sounds as well.

You can perform this procedure on just a small portion of the track as well by manually selecting it with the *Selection* tool. This can be very handy when cleaning up the beginning of the first track from an old vinyl record, where there may be more crackle than on the rest of the album.

Sometimes there will be just one irritating little pop on an otherwise pristine track that you simply can't ignore. A sound like that can usually be removed with a quick edit.

Listen to the track in Audacity, and stop playback just as you hear the offending noise. Zoom in a little, put the cursor back to just before the noise on the waveform, and listen again, stopping again just as you hear the noise. Repeat this procedure a few times until you can actually see where the noise is represented on the waveform, then place the cursor there and zoom right in to sample level—in other words, you should be able to see little dots along the waveform representing each individual digital sample.

Check both the left and right channels. If the anomaly is tiny enough, you should be able to smooth out the path using the *Draw* tool from the upper left corner to select and drag that part of the waveform more or less into line with the surrounding pattern. This takes some practice, so don't hesitate to use *Undo* frequently as you are learning.

equalization

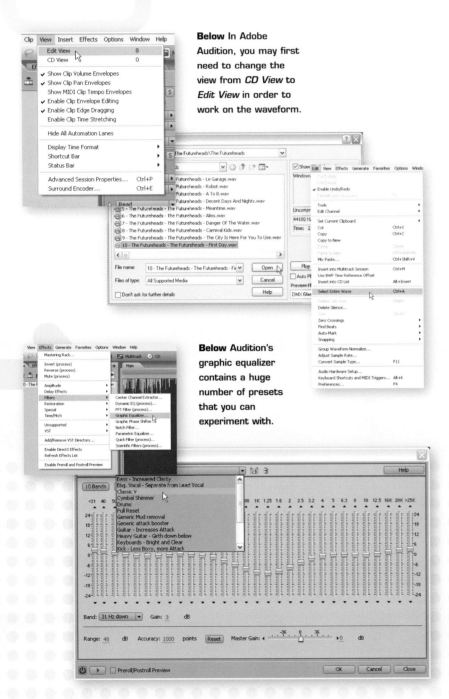

Below In Adobe Audition, you may first need to change the view from *CD View* to *Edit View* in order to work on the waveform.

Below Audition's graphic equalizer contains a huge number of presets that you can experiment with.

You can modify the equalization (EQ) settings if your recording lacks "punch" in specific frequencies. Adobe Audition offers some advanced editing tools with a simple enough interface for a beginner to grasp—a demo is available for either Mac or Windows at the Adobe website.

Upon starting Audition, you'll notice that *Multitrack* is the default interface configuration, so be sure to choose *View > Edit View* first, because this is the correct layout within which to edit a single file. The *File* menu will then allow you to open audio files—navigate to the audio file you want to edit and click *Open*. Then, choose *Edit > Select Entire Wave* to ensure that you have the entire song selected for editing.

Choosing *Effects > Filters > Graphic Equalizer* will bring up a dialog box with ten fader controls as the default selection. However, if you try out all the presets, you will see that most are set to work with the 30-band equalizer for increased accuracy. You should also take note that, for the most part, these presets are moderate—no fader is set to extremes, and if anything, greater adjustments are made when cutting rather than increasing volume. This is something to remember when you want to come up with your own settings later, but for now, select *Classic V* from the *Effect Preset* drop-down menu at the top left of the dialog box.

Make sure the *Power* button at the extreme lower left of the dialog box is green, meaning that the EQ is functional, and press the *Preview Play* button immediately to the right of it to hear the difference the EQ setting makes. You can switch the EQ on and off as the track plays to hear the significant difference the adjustment

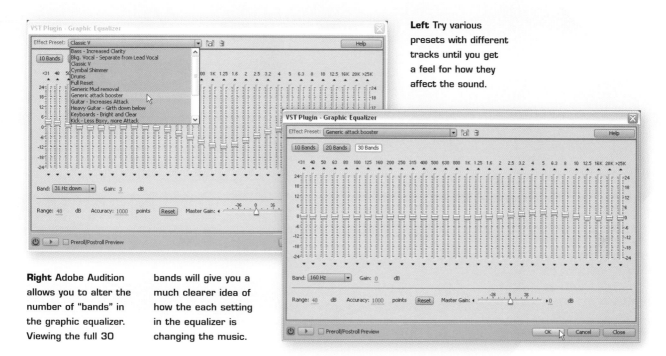

Left Try various presets with different tracks until you get a feel for how they affect the sound.

Right Adobe Audition allows you to alter the number of "bands" in the graphic equalizer. Viewing the full 30 bands will give you a much clearer idea of how the each setting in the equalizer is changing the music.

has made. The mid-range of the song has been cut, reducing the overall volume, but bringing up the low and high frequencies a bit and giving the track some "air."

Next, try the *Generic Attack Booster* preset—this is a very subtle setting. By turning the *Power* on and off with *Preview Play* enabled, you can hear how it adds brightness and punch to the overall sound.

Keep playing with the presets. Once you have found a setting you like, click *OK* to apply the EQ to your sound. Feel free to experiment with finer adjustments yourself. Remember, you can always choose *Edit > Undo* if you change your mind.

A rule of thumb with EQ is to take it easy—it can be tempting to jack up all the bass frequencies on a dance track, for example, or even to increase all levels to get a "louder" sound. Unfortunately, this will obscure sonic detail, thereby reducing the dynamic range of your track, and it

may cause the track to clip or distort. Be sure to "normalize" your track once you are done adjusting the EQ (see pages 96–97 for more on this).

The human ear can only perceive sounds in the 20Hz–20kHz range, and that is a healthy, young ear! More importantly, speakers—especially computer speakers—have a rather limited dynamic range, not only in that they stop working at certain high and low frequencies, but in the inconsistent manner in which they reproduce frequencies across the spectrum. Don't forget that virtually all stereo systems, MP3 players, and computer-based media players offer their own equalizers, that work without making permanent changes to your audio tracks. When you play a song back, you can turn it up as loud as you like, and the detail will remain intact depending on the quality of your speakers—and your ears, of course.

Above Don't be afraid to try different presets. As with most other processes, *Undo* will step back to how the track was before your edit.

volume, normalization, and limiting

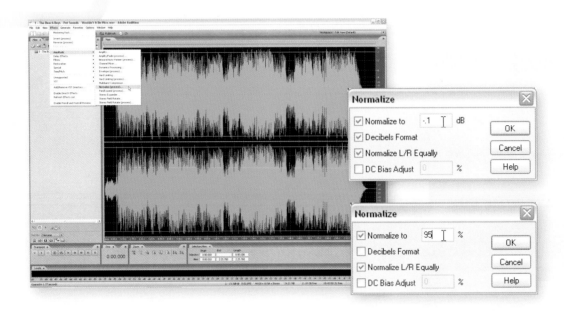

Above Virtually all audio-editing software will allow you to perform simple normalization on your tracks. Many CD-burning software packages will also allow you to do this, though they may use a different name for it.

This should be the last step in editing your audio files before converting them to MP3 or burning them to disc. Normalization ensures that a track's volume level is as high as it can be without going over 0dB, causing unpleasant-sounding digital errors known as "clipping."

Most audio-editing software will allow basic normalization, which is a very simple process. The software scans the waveform for peaks, then increases the volume of the entire file so that the highest peak does not exceed a stated limit. In Adobe Audition, simply choose *Effects > Amplitude > Normalize (process)*. If the track was not already selected, it will select the entire track by default, and you will be presented with a very simple dialog box. Digital audio professionals will usually advise that you do not select 100 percent on a 16-bit track—using a setting of about 95 percent will prevent "stray" frequencies from going

over the limit. If you opt to select the *Decibels Format* checkbox, you can enter the peak value in decibels, which should be set to -0.1dB. A fraction of a decibel will not make much difference, as one decibel is a relative measure of the smallest perceptible difference in volume.

Ensure that *Normalize L/R Equally* is selected so that both channels are kept at the same level in relation to one another, and click *OK* to begin processing. If your audio file was clipping because of EQ settings or other processing, you may see the volume level go down a little.

If you are editing digital audio files that you recorded yourself, it is possible that you managed to get the levels right, but they just sound too quiet. Sometimes, merely normalizing all your tracks may not help at all because the perceived volume is simply not high enough. While this can often be resolved in the equalization stage (see pages 94–95), it may be easier to apply "hard limiting" to the entire track in order to make it sound "louder."

Hard limiting boosts all frequencies by a set amount, but attenuates (compresses or reduces, depending on the method used by your software) frequencies that would otherwise clip. If you have ever wondered why TV commercials sound so much louder than the regular shows, it is because extreme levels of hard limiting have been used to give the ads more perceived volume and impact while still keeping them under a required decibel level. While it may sound like a good idea to use this method on all your tracks, remember that it reduces the details and the dynamics of your track, and can also increase hiss and other noise on recordings from vinyl or cassette.

To use this feature in Audition, choose *Effects > Amplitude > Hard Limiting (Process)*. In the dialog box that appears you should set *Limit Max Amplitude (volume)* to the same amount you would in the normalization process, so -0.1dB is best. The default amount for *Boost Input* is 6dB—this is high! Try 2dB instead.

Lookahead Time is the amount of time allowed for the processor to attenuate (reduce) the peaks, and *Release Time* is the amount of time allowed for the level to return to normal. These are measured in milliseconds, so the default settings of seven and 100 respectively will probably be sufficient. These rapid volume changes should be imperceptible.

Make sure *Link Left and Right* is checked, and click the *Gather Statistics Now* button. The values in *Percent Clipped* tell you how much of the audio would exceed 0dB without limiting. Change

the *Boost Input* value to 3dB and click *Gather Statistics Now* again—note the higher percentages. Test your track using the *Preview* button, and when you are satisfied, click *OK*.

As with EQ, hard limiting is usually best kept to a minimum, as every music player has a volume control, and excessive processing usually reduces the musical detail in a track, even if it gives the amateur digital audio enthusiast a thrill to make "everything louder than everything else." Moreover, it can be jarring for random tracks on one album to burst forth with much higher volume levels than others, a phenomenon that may be indicated by the worn Mute button on your television remote control.

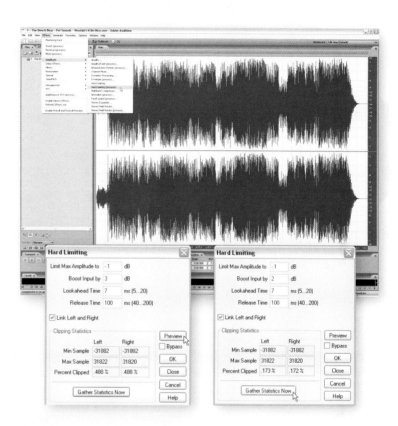

Above Hard limiting can be used to boost all of the frequencies in a track, making it sound louder without actually increasing the volume.

converting to MP3

While many compressed file formats are fighting for attention (see pages 90–91), MP3 is the reigning champion, and as such it is also the format that is most compatible with all personal music devices and computer-based digital audio players. The main reason you will want to convert to MP3, however, is to save on space—if storage space was unlimited, it would make more sense just to keep all files in an uncompressed format, because the quality

Below Apple's iTunes software is a fully featured music management package that is just as useful for people without iPods or Macs.

would remain pristine. MP3 is "lossy" compression, so once the conversion is made you will not want to edit the audio file in any way, as this can increase otherwise imperceptible flaws brought about through the compression process.

There are many file converters available, with Apple's iTunes being a popular choice as it is freely downloadable, easy to use, and works on both Windows and Mac systems. In addition, iTunes is the intended software for use with iPods (see pages 104–105).

For audiophiles on a tight budget, CDex is a good choice for the Windows platform, and Audion works very well with all Mac versions. Both of these products are free, but remember, free software often does not come with technical support.

If you intend to burn tracks to a CD, you should skip ahead to Creating CDs (pages 100–103). While you can burn CDs from MP3 files, you will achieve better quality results if you use original WAV or AIFF files.

To convert files using iTunes, simply open the application and choose *Edit > Preferences*. Select the *Advanced* tab, then select the *Importing* tab within the secondary window. Since you are converting to MP3, choose *MP3 Encoder* from the *Import Using* drop-down menu.

Select *Custom* from the *Setting* drop-down menu—the dialog box that appears will allow you to optimize settings in order to get the smallest files with the highest possible quality. The minimum *Stereo Bit Rate* you should consider for quality music files is 128kbps—this is just below CD-quality and should be used when drive space is at a premium. 192kbps is a good setting for high-quality MP3 files if storage

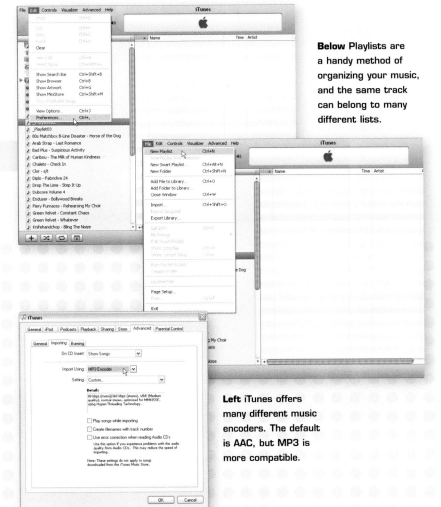

Below Playlists are a handy method of organizing your music, and the same track can belong to many different lists.

Left iTunes offers many different music encoders. The default is AAC, but MP3 is more compatible.

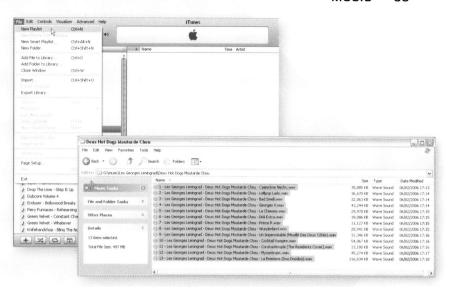

is not as much of a consideration. Because the iTunes encoder allows Variable Bit Rate (VBR) encoding, 160kbps with VBR enabled is a good choice—this will ensure a minimum bitrate of 160kbps while VBR encoding will increase the bitrate slightly during more complex passages of music. As with bitrate, choose a VBR quality setting that corresponds to the amount of space you have available.

Auto settings for *Sample Rate* and *Channels* will suffice as long as your files were recorded properly, because this will duplicate the settings of the original file, that should be stereo with a sample rate of 44.1kHz. *Stereo Mode* should remain at *Normal*; *Joint Stereo* is intended for lower-quality files.

Deselect the *Smart Encoding Adjustments* checkbox unless you want iTunes to modify your settings based on your source audio. *Filter Frequencies Below 10Hz* can be checked, because this may eliminate some inaudible information from the audio file. When you are done, click *OK*.

Encoding will be faster if you do not play the songs while iTunes is importing them. Do not let iTunes create filenames on its own if you have already painstakingly devised a long, detailed filename for each track as they may be truncated—this can be a useful setting if you are importing directly from CD, however. Speaking of which, if you experience digital "pops" or glitches in the resulting MP3 files when converting directly from CD, enable *Error Correction* in this window. Click *OK* when you are done modifying your settings.

Next, create a new playlist by choosing *File > New Playlist*—normally you will want to name it after the artist

name and the album title. Navigate to the folder containing your original audio files and select all of the files that you want to convert. If the playlist is selected, drag the files onto the empty iTunes window—or, to ensure that they end up in the correct playlist, drop them onto the playlist's title in the window on the left.

Every file should now appear in your iTunes window. Select them all and choose *Advanced > Convert Selection to MP3*. The files will be converted and saved in the iTunes folder specified under *Edit > Preferences > Advanced > General*.

Above Using iTunes, it's very simple to convert a whole group of WAV or AIFF files into MP3s at once by adding them to a playlist.

creating CDs and DVDs

To play digital music files on your stereo system or in your car, you may need to burn them to a CD-R. All recent desktop computers include a CD writing drive, and while it is likely that CD burning capability is built into your operating system, using specialized software to do this can give you more control over the settings—and, sometimes, better quality results.

Remember, if your files are in uncompressed WAV or AIFF format, writing them to an audio CD is merely a transfer of data. There is no loss of quality unlike recording to an audio cassette. However, if your files are in MP3 or some other compressed format, the file size will increase in the conversion to CD audio files, but the audio quality will not. It is best, therefore, to use uncompressed audio files.

Your CD-burner may have dedicated software, such as Roxio Easy Media Creator or Nero, but you should also be able to use any software that plays music. ITunes works well for this purpose.

To begin, insert a blank CD-R in the appropriate drive, and start iTunes. The software may then open a dialog box with instructions on how to burn your CD and how to create a new playlist (see pages 106–109). If so, click *OK*. Select the playlist you want to burn to disc; the number of songs, the total time of the playlist, and the number of megabytes taken up by the audio files will be displayed under the track-listing window.

A CD can contain approximately 74 minutes of music, equivalent to 650MB of data. Some software may allow you to burn up to 700MB of data on a CD-R, but ordinary CD players may have trouble reading these discs. Also, don't be fooled— your MP3 files can be burned to disc, but unless otherwise specified they will be converted to CD audio format. 74 minutes of music will fill an entire disc even if your source files are much smaller.

It is worth noting, however, that many of the latest CD players are capable of playing CD-Rs containing MP3 data—that is, MP3 files that have not been converted to CD audio. You will need to check the documentation for your CD player to find out if this is possible; if so, it will allow you to burn as many MP3-encoded songs as you can fit onto a 650MB disc.

Left Most music-management software can also burn CDs, and iTunes is no exception. If you want to play the CD back on a standard stereo system, then make sure you burn the music as an *Audio CD*.

Right Both PCs and Macs can be set to automatically bring up an audio CD-burning prompt when a blank disc is inserted.

Above and right Once you have constructed a playlist in your music-management software, you can use it to burn CDs containing the music tracks. MP3 CDs will only contain the MP3 files themselves, and therefore will not be listenable to on a standard hi-fi system. You can change the type of CD that is burned in the *Preferences* window.

creating CDs and DVDs continued

Choose *Edit > Preferences* from the top menu, then choose the *Burning* sub-tab under the *Advanced* tab. Your preferred speed should always be set to *Maximum Possible* unless your drive is one of the older, error-prone models. Then, you can choose between an Audio CD, which will play on any CD player; an MP3 CD, which will only play on computer drives, or on consumer drives that explicitly feature that capability; or, a Data CD, that—like the MP3 CD—merely copies data byte-for-byte to the CD without converting it to CD audio format. Data CDs containing uncompressed files will play on computers, but not on anything else, so do not use this setting unless you are creating a backup copy of your music files.

If you are burning an Audio CD, you may want to insert gaps of silence between tracks, but this is generally not necessary. Enabling *Sound Check* will cause iTunes to adjust the volume of all your files to about the same level. You might have done this already during the normalization process (see pages 96–97), but if not, you may want to check this box. This may have undesirable consequences in that pieces of intentionally quieter music may suddenly become louder when burned to CD, so beware—you can only record to a CD-R once. Once you are satisfied with your settings, click *OK*.

Ensure that the little box to the left of each of the tracks you want to burn from your selected playlist is checked, and make sure all the checked songs are in the correct order; then, click *Burn Disc* in the upper-right corner. iTunes will display a progress indicator with the track currently being burned and the estimated time remaining until the CD is ready. If the amount of music exceeds the amount of space on one disc, iTunes will automatically ask you to insert another CD-R. Remember: if you cancel the process or eject the disc in mid-progress, your disc will no longer be of much use to anyone, except perhaps as a drink coaster.

If you have a drive that supports writing to DVD, the procedure for burning to a DVD-R disc is the same as it is for a CD-R, except that you will have a whopping 4.7GB of space and the ability to fit about five times as many songs on one disc! Note that many consumer drives will not recognize rewritable media such as CD-RW, DVD-RW and DVD+RW discs, though your computer probably will.

Also note that as the DVD format war rages on, most DVD-writing drives will label themselves as "DVD±RW compatible"—this simply means that they can write to both DVD-RW ("dash") and DVD+RW ("plus") media. The main difference between the two formats is that while DVD-RW must be written to in one sweep, like a CD-RW, you can write bits of data to DVD+RW discs in the same way as you would a regular hard drive. However, DVD+RW media tends to be more expensive.

THE FUTURE OF DISC FORMATS

Although MP3 players are an efficient means of listening to music on the go, the disc format is not likely to disappear anytime soon. There is a great deal of debate as to whether most people can even hear the difference between CD audio and the new, ultra-high-quality formats such as SACD and DVD-Audio. An untrained ear will certainly not perceive any difference—despite this, the battle to take over the future of the market has begun.

SACD: The Super Audio CD format is a new format that relies on Direct Stream Digital (DSD) technology instead of PCM (see page 91 for more on PCM), using small 1-bit samples at a high sampling rate of 2.8224 megahertz—remember, CD audio uses larger 16-bit samples and a lower sampling rate of 44.1kHz (0.00441MHz). SACD audio can be mixed for stereo or for "multi-channel" mixes, including—but not limited to—5.1 surround sound (see pages 112–113). This format uses a series of complex processes that enable a wider dynamic range (higher treble and lower bass) and better frequency response (more accurate playback of all highs and lows).

DVD-Audio: The main competitor to SACD, using LPCM encoding (losslessly compressed version of PCM) of 24-bit samples at 192kHz in stereo, and lower sample rates for surround sound mixes, both of which can be included even on a single disc. Although these can only be decoded by special players, hybrid DVD-Audio discs (HDADs) offer a separate DVD-Audio mix alongside a regular DVD-quality mix (24-bit/96kHz) that can be played on any DVD machine.

DualDisc: Contains standard CD-quality audio alongside higher-quality DVD-Audio-based mixes.

DVD Plus: European equivalent to DualDisc.

HD DVD: High-Definition DVDs are a new physical format that uses a short-wavelength blue-violet laser to read a higher density of data than the original red laser on conventional DVD and CD players. This will increase the capacity of a single disc.

BD: Blu-ray Discs are the main competitor to HD DVDs. Both are primarily related to movies, but will affect the amount and quality of audio available on a single disc.

iPods and MP3 players

Right The most
well-known name
in personal music
players is undoubtedly
the Apple iPod, but
there are numerous
other devices available
with different features
and different price
points. Shop around
until you find a player
that fits the way you
want to use it.

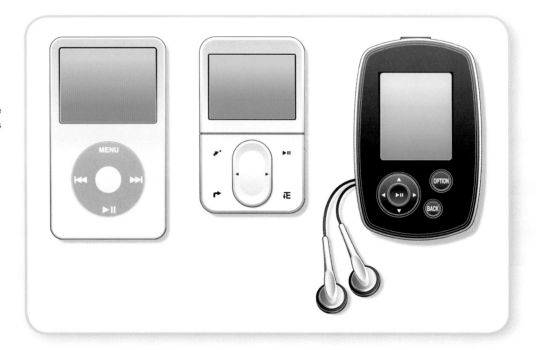

THE FUTURE OF MP3

Innovations in the MP3 format have been driven by the raging
success of MP3 players. For example, the patented MP3 encoder
developed by Fraunhofer IIS—the inventors of the format—is the
standard for commercial software. However, an open-source
encoder called **LAME** (Lame Ain't an MP3 Encoder) is now being
used in many digital audio applications due to the fact that
developers do not need to pay a patent to use it.

MP3pro is a new standard developed by Coding Technologies.
They have introduced a concept called Spectral Band Replication
(SBR), a further development in perceptual audio compression
that has apparently reduced the size of some MP3 files by
about one half, although this requires a special decoder during
playback. One would expect further developments of this type
as the industry for portable music players continues to grow.

It is rare to take a journey on the public
transit of any major metropolitan center
without seeing the meandering white wires
of the ubiquitous iPod earbuds, though
this was certainly not the first portable
device to store and play back MP3 files
through a set of headphones. While the
iPod and other high-capacity players—such
as the Cowon iAudio, the Creative Labs
ZEN, and the Toshiba Gigabeat—are
drive-based devices, the first MP3 players
employed flash memory.

While drive-based devices actually
use tiny hard drives and are subject
to skipping, flash memory is a form
of EEPROM (Electrically-Erasable
Programmable Read-Only Memory) and
relies on no moving parts. This is similar

to the RAM (Random Access Memory) chips in your computer, except that flash memory chips are non-volatile: they can retain data without the need of a power supply. This technology is still popular for smaller players with capacities measured in megabytes rather than gigabytes, although many of these have breached the one-GB limit, such as Creative Labs' popular MuVo or the latest Mobiblu DAH devices—or, most notably, another Apple product called the iPod Nano that boasts capacities of up to 4GB.

No matter which product you purchase, it will include some form of software—such as a driver to allow the computer to recognize it when you plug it in, at the very least—allowing you to access and modify the songs on the device. The iPod is designed to use iTunes software for updates, although third-party software does exist for Apple devices.

Speaking of updates, most hard-drive-based players will have operating systems of their own, and these often need to be updated by plugging into a computer with Internet access and downloading update software from the manufacturer's website. Operating systems—and larger screens—have become necessary as many of these players can now hold digital photos, digital video, and other computer files, or offer calendar-based personal organization features.

In contrast, most flash-memory-based players will simply allow you to plug them directly into a USB port, and will behave just like another drive on your computer, so you can simply drag and drop files onto them at whim.

USB VERSUS FIREWIRE

Front-located USB and FireWire ports on desktop computers are extremely convenient for connecting your personal music player, but if you do not have these, you can usually purchase extension cables that will plug into the back of your machine, making these ports more accessible.

USB (Universal Serial Bus) 2.0

USB cables support a top speed of 480 megabits per second if they support the 2.0 standard. Older devices may only support the 1.1 standard of 12Mbps, but this is usually sufficient for certain types of devices, such as keyboards. Multiple devices can be "chained" together into one port, for example a mouse can plug into a keyboard that plugs into the computer.

FireWire or IEEE 1394 or i.Link

Although USB 2.0 was supposed to be faster than the earliest version of FireWire (400), which allowed data transfers of up to about 400Mbps, sustained transfers (such as from a portable music device) tended to be faster via FireWire 400. In addition, a newer version—FireWire 800—boasts transfer rates of almost 800Mbps, and when the full specification becomes more commonly implemented in new computers, data transfer rates of about 3.2 gigabits per second will be possible. The reason there are usually several more USB ports than FireWire on new computers is that manufacturers must pay a royalty on each system that uses IEEE 1394 due to patents held by Apple, Sony, and other companies.

The Apple devices are certainly well designed, and this stylish look is a major part of their popularity. However, do not hesitate to shop around and read the reviews on the Web, because you might find a device that suits you just as well— or possibly better—for a lower price.

maintaining a music library

Below When storing music on your computer solely by filename, it can be difficult to sort the tracks by different criteria—even if you have been very careful in your naming.

As your digital music collection grows, file organization will become a serious issue if you neglect it. Most people will become frustrated skipping through hundreds of tracks just to find an elusive old favorite with a completely irrelevant file name. Just as with your other computer files, make sure you establish a well-ordered folder system from the beginning.

You will also find that MP3 players and other devices are not suited to long filenames. For this reason, MP3 files can contain metadata—meaning "data about data"—to identify them on computers and portable devices. The most widespread standard for this type of information is called ID3 (short for Identify an MP3), and this data can be appended to OGG, AAC, WMA, and other files, in addition to MP3s. Some uncompressed files, such as WAVs, do not support metadata.

Adding this information to a file is called tagging, and depending on the version of the standard recognized by your software media player or audio device, this usually includes the song title, the artist name, the album the song is from, the year it was released, and the genre of music. It can also include the songwriter name (as this often differs from the artist[s] who performed the track), copyright information, lyrics (if any), digital rights data, sound information, and even a digital image—the album artwork, for example.

Your operating system will let you view and/or edit metadata in most files (Cmd+I on a Mac, or right-click and select *Properties* in Windows), but it is easier to

Right MP3 metadata can contain a huge variety of information, from the obvious—such as artist and album—to the more obscure—such as beats per minute.

do this using some kind of media software, such as iTunes. Select the track you want to edit in the main window and choose *File > Get Info* from the top menu. A dialog box will appear with all the information on that track.

The track's *Summary* contains a combination of general file information, metadata saved within the file itself, and information iTunes keeps for sorting purposes, such as how often the track has been played. Clicking the *Info* tab allows you to edit the track information in the fields provided. Save your changes by clicking *OK*.

M3U FILES

MPEG Version 3.0 URL (M3U) files contain information on the location— on the local hard drive or over the Internet—of a group of files. Originally the native playlist file format of a popular Windows-based MP3 player called Winamp, most media players can read these basic text files, although some cannot edit or save them.

Right iTunes' *Get Info* window displays a handy summary of all of the information that is available for the selected track, including album cover art.

Left By clicking on the *Info* tab, you can not only view the information present, but also edit it if anything is incorrect.

maintaining a music library continued

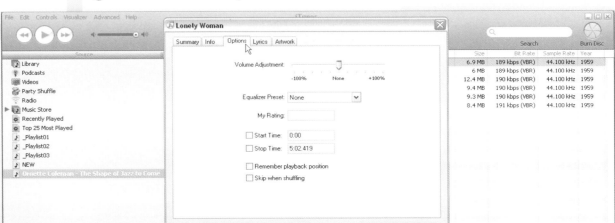

Above The *Options* tab in iTunes allows you to specify certain playback settings for each track. This means, for example, that you can specify an equalizer preset to use with the track without having to change the audio data of the track itself.

The *Options* tab reveals a variety of non-permanent modifications you can make to the track that will only be recognized by iTunes or an iPod. These settings can be very handy if you aren't comfortable editing the audio in any permanent manner with software. The *Remember Playback Position* setting is useful when taking a break from a long podcast (see pages 114–117) as it will help the player "remember" where you last left off.

The *Lyrics* and *Artwork* tabs can accommodate text and graphics, but not all software or media players will be able to recognize these, and you may find that certain files cannot contain this information.

As you can imagine, it can become rather tedious editing the information in every single file. It is for this reason that the Gracenote CDDB (Compact Disc Database) exists. When a CD has been inserted into the drive on your computer, media players like iTunes or Windows Media Player will attempt to access this database over the Web in order to match the data on the disc with a set of related information

stored in the database. If a match is found, the information will be downloaded and applied to the CD in the drive, and if you choose to rip the songs to your hard drive, the ripping software can not only name the files, but can add appropriate metadata to them automatically.

You can also force this procedure in iTunes by choosing *Advanced > Get CD Track Names*. As the database is built from the efforts of music lovers around the world, you can also *Submit CD Track Names* if a CD you own has not been submitted yet.

To create playlists and custom compilations from your music collection, you do not have to move or copy files from their original locations on your hard drive—simply create them in iTunes or another application and let the software keep track of where they are. iTunes stores a link to each music file registered with it, and updates the link when the music file is moved or deleted. You can add one song to multiple playlists in this manner without having to actually duplicate the file.

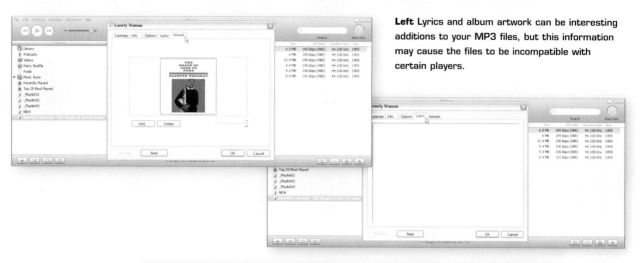

Left Lyrics and album artwork can be interesting additions to your MP3 files, but this information may cause the files to be incompatible with certain players.

Right The Gracenote CDDB database is an incredibly useful resource, allowing you to download track and album information at the click of a button, rather than tediously entering it all yourself.

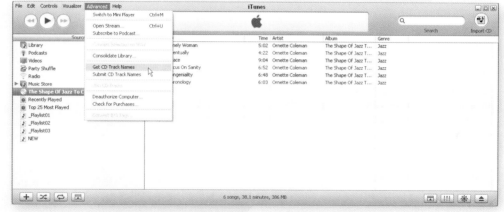

Left On the rare occasions that the Gracenote database doesn't contain information for the CD you're ripping, then add the information yourself and submit it to Gracenote.

buying tracks on the Internet

The most remarkable manner in which the MP3 file format has transformed the music industry is in the purchasing of individual tracks over the Web. While CD singles are popular in the U.K., they are less so in North America, where the overwhelming majority of CDs in chain stores are albums. This creates a problem in that people who like one track may not want to purchase an entire album to hear it.

Buying tracks over the Internet not only allows the customer to choose individual songs from an album, but also to quickly and easily sample the tracks before making a purchase. In addition, free MP3 downloads from artist or record label websites have proven to work as promotional and marketing tools before an album's release or a concert tour.

Hardcore music fans really love the ability to purchase tracks from foreign artists that have been released in other countries before anyone else has heard them. There are no import surcharges associated with the purchase and online shops are never out of stock. Moreover, Web commerce gives smaller labels and independent artists an advantage and allows them to compete on the same level as huge entertainment companies.

Best of all, there is no need to leave your home or office when purchasing MP3s, and purchased music can be enjoyed the moment the download has completed.

Of course, some music lovers or collectors just want to own the better quality CD, and many DJs still rely on 12-inch vinyl singles. Plus, there is a

Right There are a huge number of sites on the Internet that enable you to purchase and legally download music tracks. These are cheap—often around 99 cents per track—and usually contain lots of obscure bands that you wouldn't find in a traditional music store.

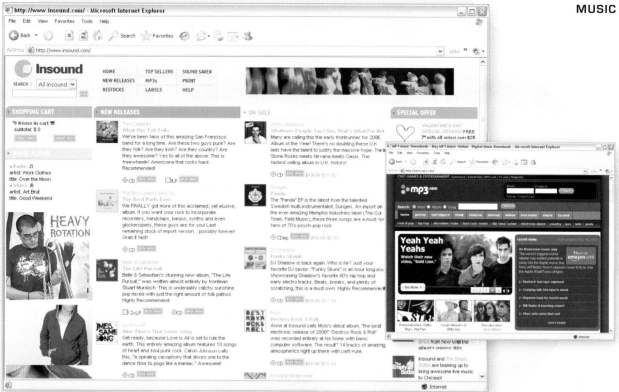

dark side to this revolution, and it is the problem of piracy. Digital data is easily copied and transmitted over the Internet, and despite the best efforts of the music industry and software makers, early versions of digital rights management standards have not slowed the illegal transfer of files one bit. However, many of the unauthorized MP3 files available are poorly or improperly encoded. Some artists have even "leaked" bogus editions of albums before they have been released, embedded with recorded messages or other surprises instead of the expected material. As you would expect, these have worked very well as prerelease promotion.

Windows Media Player and iTunes both allow users to access libraries of music over the Web with their own online shops, but by using your browser you can access dozens of other sites to suit every conceivable musical taste. For example,

www.mp3.com has been around for ages and offers a good general range of music.

For more adventurous listeners, www.insound.com is a good choice— they offer a huge collection of free, full-length MP3 samples to download as well. www.karmadownload.com is a good choice to find quirky music from up-and-coming European artists, some of which is not even available in CD format.

All online MP3 shops offer shortened samples of the music, so you will never have to worry that you are about to purchase the wrong track or one that you might not like. But with the prices at only about 99 cents per song, you can afford to experiment a little!

Be sure to visit your favorite artists' websites often, because most will offer free MP3 downloads from time to time, and these can sometimes be exclusive or unreleased tracks that will not be made available for purchase.

Above Most online stores allow you to listen to preview versions of the songs. These are normally 30-second clips that are recorded in a low-quality compression format to prevent you from just downloading the preview. Don't worry, though, the actual track will be presented to you at full quality when you purchase it.

playing digital music in your home

Right A standard
5.1 speaker system
contains 5 standard
speakers—front left,
front right, rear
left, rear right, and
front center—and
a subwoofer for
providing extra
bass boost.

If you are planning to listen to digital audio stored on your computer, the first thing you will need is a decent set of speakers—ordinary computer speakers will not cut it. There are an enormous number of possibilities and a correspondingly wide range of prices, so shopping around will be a necessity. Ideally, you should bring a CD of music that you enjoy into a shop so that you can hear how it sounds though a set of speakers before you buy them.

If space is at a premium, make sure the speakers you purchase are shielded—this means the magnetic field produced by the speakers is dampened so that you can place them near a monitor without causing visual distortion on the screen.

A subwoofer is a nice addition to boost bass sounds, but make sure your sound card supports it. Many digital file formats do support surround sound, as do many sound cards, so this is an option if you are interested. The most common 5.1 surround system includes two sets of right and left speakers for front and side, a front-center speaker, and a subwoofer for low frequencies—the ".1" refers to the subwoofer. A 4.1 system omits the front-center speaker. A 6.1 system is the same as 5.1, but with an additional rear-center speaker, and a 7.1 system has left and right rear speakers. You should buy your entire set together so that each speaker's dynamic range complements the others.

The subwoofer should be placed on the floor—anywhere is fine, as bass sound is non-directional—and your main right and left speakers should be at ear level. If your room has many flat, hard surfaces, this can make your music sound tinny. Curtains, carpeting, soft furniture and pillows can help to mellow it.

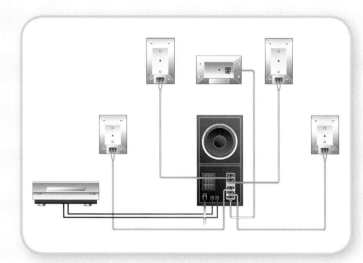

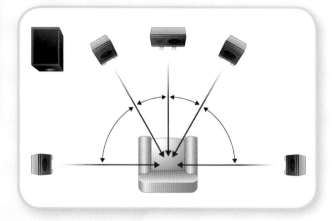

Below Carefully consider where the speakers in your surround-sound system will go in your room. The subwoofer is non-directional, but all other speakers should be directed toward you at ear-level.

Above Surround-sound systems can require huge amounts of cabling. It's worth considering where all this cable will go at the same time as you're planning on purchasing and installing a system.

If you have a roommate or a spouse who does not share your taste for glitchcore or experimental free jazz, you may want to invest in a quality set of headphones. Headphone pads that press against your ears are not very comfortable for prolonged listening, so it is a good idea to invest in a decent pair of circumaural headphones—with pads that fit around your ears—preferably with noise cancelling ability. This will prevent you from having to turn up the volume to unsafe levels just to drown out background sounds.

To hear music through your speakers, the digital data in an audio file must be converted to an analog signal. The accuracy with which this signal is converted depends on the quality of your sound card, so you should take the trouble to purchase a decent model. Sound cards are no longer as expensive as they used to be—good quality consumer cards with remote controls specifically made for music lovers can now be had for under $100. If you are on a laptop, there are still plenty of terrific USB-based sound cards available, and most of these feature Line-In jacks. If you own a turntable, be sure to look for a card with a turntable preamp built in (see pages 80–81).

Many companies boast about their cards' support for 24-bit sound with frequencies of up to 192kHz, but as the consumer standard is still CD-quality audio (16-bit sample depth at 44.1kHz; see pages 90–91), this is overkill—it cannot increase the quality of your audio in any way. However, as it is becoming difficult to find cards that do not support 24-bit audio, you might just have to consider it an investment in the future.

Internet radio and podcasts

Right RealPlayer was one of the first popular streaming audio applications, and it is still in wide use today.

In the same way that digital audio file compression has revolutionized the way music is bought and sold (see pages 110–111), it has also democratized the way music is broadcast. Thousands of radio stations around the world offer live audio streams—audio data that can be listened to as it is downloaded—so that anyone in the world can listen to them, but there are also numerous unregulated, Internet-only stations. This is because audio file compression has reduced the size of the files, enabling them to be transferred much more quickly over the Web.

Several independent news sources offer their radio programming over the Web, including National Public Radio in the U.S., the BBC in the U.K., and the CBC in Canada. The NPR is broadcast in Real Audio so the RealPlayer is required, although they also offer downloadable podcasts. The BBC has a custom player built into a Web page. Finally, the CBC uses Windows Media Player, which is available for both Windows and Mac. All of these stations offer diverse music programming. College, university and

Left One advantage of Internet radio stations is that they can be accessed from anywhere in the world with a good enough Internet connection. You need never be away from your favorite station again!

Left Different radio stations use different methods of broadcasting data. Most, however, offer an alternative if you can't use the primary streaming method.

community radio stations all over the world also offer live webcasts if you are interested in independent music or local information from a smaller specific region. Many music-management programs, such as iTunes, contain lists of Internet radio webcasts.

London's Resonance 104.4 FM offers a superb online radio station—unlike many other stations, they managed to start on the Web and migrate to terrestrial radio. Supported by the London Musicians' Collective, it offer a huge range of musical and artistic programming that you are unlikely to hear on any other station. They are also one of the few stations to offer webcasts in OGG Vorbis (see pages 90–91), as well as in several other formats.

As you could guess from the pink and plastic interface of their website, Club977 is known primarily as a popular source of

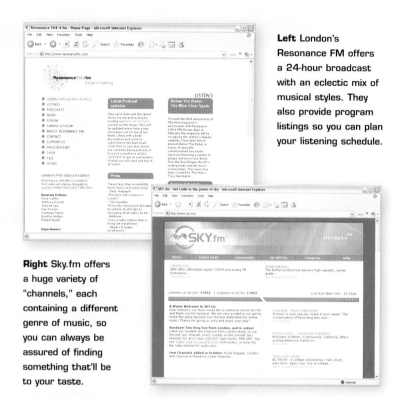

Left London's Resonance FM offers a 24-hour broadcast with an eclectic mix of musical styles. They also provide program listings so you can plan your listening schedule.

Right Sky.fm offers a huge variety of "channels," each containing a different genre of music, so you can always be assured of finding something that'll be to your taste.

Left and below Club 977 focuses on one very specific genre— '80s music! You can log on to get your '80s fix at any time, night or day.

Internet radio and podcasts continued

Right Instead of going to the website and trying to find a station to listen to, many sites now provide "podcasts" that can be listened to directly from music managers, such as iTunes. Inside iTunes, you can subscribe to a podcast to make sure that you have the most recent edition of the broadcast.

Left There are a huge number of podcasts available, covering not only music of all genres, but also spoken-word material, such as comedy.

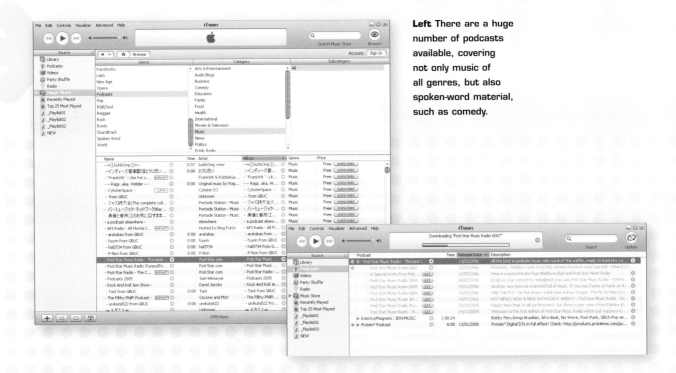

streamed '80s pop music. However, they offer a range of stations for other genres, such as current Top 40, and popular country—not bad for a former pirate radio station based in Florida. Sky.fm offers an even wider range of broadcasting, including classical, new age, roots reggae, '70s, dance, ambient, lounge, and much more.

Podcasting has also changed the way people listen to music; this entails putting a recorded broadcast on the Web for anyone to download and listen to. The name is derived from the idea that the recorded material can be transferred to an iPod or other personal audio device.

The easiest method for finding this type of content is by using the iTunes podcast directory, that can be accessed by selecting *Podcasts* from the menu on the left, then clicking the *Podcast Directory* link under the main window. Click on the *Browse* link under the *Inside the Music Store* menu—make sure *Podcasts* is selected from the drop-down menu—and the screen will change to a browsing interface. Select *Podcasts* from the *Browse* menu, *Music* from the *Category* menu, and finally, *All* from the *Subcategory* menu. A list of available podcasts will load in the window below. You will see that there are no limits on content or language, which is what makes the world of podcasting so exciting! Even better—the vast majority of these are absolutely free of charge.

Upon subscribing to a podcast, you will be returned to the *Podcasts* menu in iTunes, where an episode of the chosen show will download while you wait. Click on the arrow to the immediate left of the podcast title, and you will be able to see a list of episodes and other content, that you can *Get* whenever you choose. Clicking on the arrow to the immediate

right of the title will open that podcaster's website. The subscription is not a binding agreement—you can unsubscribe at any time, and either keep or delete the episodes you have already downloaded.

Both webcasting and podcasting are very easy to do, and there are now special, relatively low, international webcast licensing fees meaning that anyone with an Internet connection can host an online radio show. If you are feeling the urge to enlighten the rest of the world with your impeccable tastes in music, a good place to begin is at SHOUTcast, where complete instructions for setting up your own streaming radio station are provided along with links to the relevant licensing organizations. Plus, sites where "podsafe" music—tracks provided by the artists under a special licence that allows it to be rebroadcast by anyone—are also a good starting point if you want to set up your own podcast.

Below Nullsoft's SHOUTcast service allows you to set up your own Internet radio station. It also contains a directory of the stations currently available, that you can listen to at your leisure.

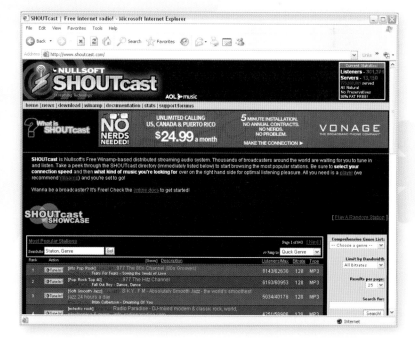

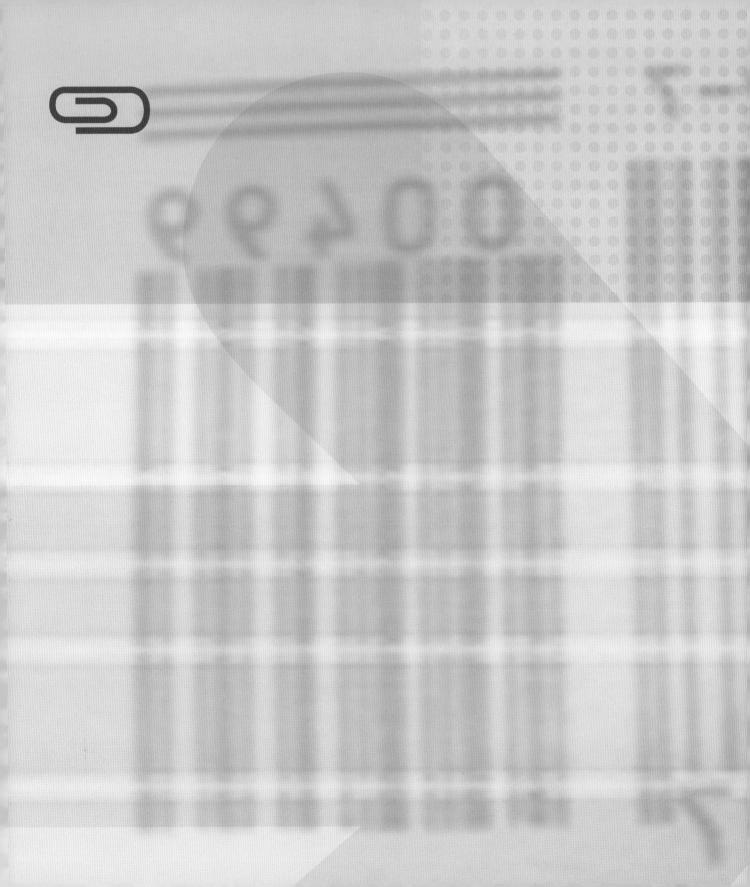

section four
documents

scanners

Scanners are useful for getting things from the real world into your computer. There are many different kinds of scanner available, and their prices range from the affordable (for example under $100) to the incredibly expensive ($35,000+). Most people certainly don't need anything remotely near the top end of the market, but you might be a little disappointed by the results you get from the very cheapest models.

When you buy a scanner you'll need to make sure it comes with the appropriate interface and software for your computer. Most devices will connect using USB although a few offer FireWire interfaces or, in specialist or dated cases, SCSI (Small Computer System Interface). Unless you know you need something specific, go for USB every time.

Below Scanners can do more than just transfer images to your computer. They can also be used to read text documents using OCR, or even scan sheets of music in an editable format.

You should also make sure the bundled software is compatible with your computer's operating system. Not every scanner will work with both Mac OS and Windows, and not all that do will work with the most recent OS versions. Most will, of course, but it is always worth checking these details.

You'll need to get the right kind of scanner for your needs, too. Most scanners are simple "flatbed" devices which have a Letter-sized glass panel and a simple lid. This acts very much like a photocopier, bouncing light off what you place on the glass and recording what it sees as an image file on your computer, whether it is a photo, a recipe, or a birth certificate. Others are specialist slide scanning devices, great for capturing negatives and slides but no good at all for scanning prints. If you have a lot of slides to scan these are worth considering. Otherwise, flatbed scanners with transparency scanning attachments can do a fair job.

Many budget-friendly scanners have shortcut buttons arranged along their fronts that trigger different kinds of scanning tuned for different uses. These usually automate the entire process, delivering a finished scan with no more input from you. Scanning for print, for e-mail or Web, and for basic archiving

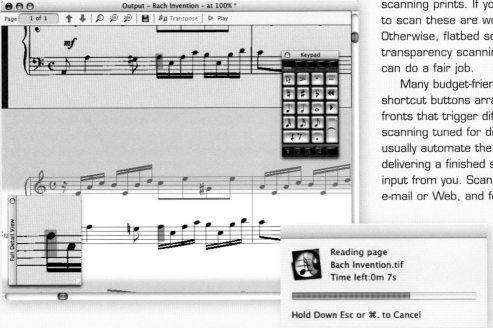

all demand slightly different settings to work well, and these shortcuts can save a lot of time and head-scratching. There will be similar easy-scan options in the scanner software itself, so you can do this from there if you want just a little more control. If this still isn't enough for you, see Scanner Settings on pages 122–123 for more in-depth information.

OCR

Some flatbed scanners have sheet-feeder attachments so you can stack up a collection of pages and have them scanned in, one after the other, more or less automatically. This is particularly useful if you use your scanner for OCR (optical character recognition) work, translating the words on a printed page into editable text on the computer and saving you hours of dull retyping. In many cases they'll even do a fair job of recognizing and scanning text columns and graphics and reassembling a layout, but don't rely on this working consistently.

OCR software is sometimes bundled with a scanner, so check what's included if that's of real interest. If you don't get OCR software with your scanner you can buy it separately; for example the relatively affordable TextBridge Pro and the powerful but expensive OmniPage Pro are well known in this field.

The success rate of using OCR depends entirely on the quality and makeup of your originals. Clear, clean typeset columns of text at a reasonable size will always work out better than faded faxes and fifth-generation photocopies. Odd typefaces can cause problems, although modern OCR software is pretty smart. With the

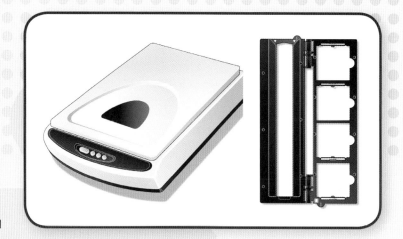

usual OCR package's combination of letter recognition and built-in dictionaries, it will generally be about 98–99 percent accurate with simple documents—that's 99 percent of characters, not words, so be prepared to do a small amount of correction work afterwards.

The software may work entirely automatically or it may have an interactive mode where you'll be asked to lend a hand in making decisions about unclear letter shapes. The scanned results will usually be saved in a word-processor format or a plain text document, ready for you to check and edit yourself. If you only need to import a paragraph or two on the odd occasion, using OCR may be overkill. On the other hand, if you need to deal with transcribing documents regularly or you just have one big task to do, for example importing a big research paper, there's no doubt that OCR software will save you enormous amounts of time.

Above Many scanners come with attachments for scanning photographic negatives and slides. There will also usually be a setting on the scanner that will need to be changed to make sure that it scans these correctly. Consult the manual that shipped with the scanner for more information.

scanner settings

Your scanner software will have a set of simple choices for the kind of scanning you want to do. If these deliver the right results then stick with them, but if you want more hands-on control you'll need to understand a little more about what is involved with making a good scan.

The most important thing to understand when choosing custom scanner settings is image resolution. This is all about "pixels per inch" (often called dots per inch). Scans are made up of tiny squares of colors—the pixels—in a regular grid. The tinier the squares, the more detail the scan can hold—but with tinier squares (more pixels per inch), the graphic will take more room on your disk and take longer to print and to e-mail to someone. The trick is to scan something so that it has enough resolution for what you want, but no more. If you're

Below Although you can make a great deal of alterations when you first scan your image, it's often better—if you have time—to scan at default and make all the alterations in your image-editing software.

scanning something just to show it on screen it doesn't need to be captured with nearly as much detail as when you want to use it in a print. 72 pixels per inch is perfect; if your scanner offers 75ppi that's close enough.

If you want to print scans that look as good as the originals, aim for at least 200ppi and preferably 300ppi or so. Anything lower, and details will start to be lost. For scanning and printing documents with type or other kinds of sharp, fine lines, the image you scan should be at least 300ppi and preferably higher.

Where this can get a little more complicated is when you want to enlarge or reduce the original. If you scan a picture at 300ppi but then print it out at twice the size, you're simply enlarging the pixels along with the image. The result is an image printed at an 150 "effective" pixels per inch; you've stretched the 300 per inch to cover twice as much space. Don't worry too much about the math of all this, just get a feel for the basic logic so you won't end up with images that are too crude and blocky or so large that they take an age to print.

With originals that don't need to be captured in color, you should scan in grayscale mode or black and white to save memory. It takes only a third as much memory to work with a grayscale image as it does a full color one, and pure black-and-white graphics take 1/24th as much space as color. Do remember that black-and-white scans are less forgiving of low resolutions; they show pixelated edges in stark, high-contrast relief. OCR scanning software normally captures pages in very high resolution black and

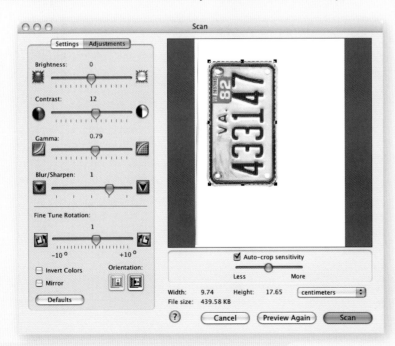

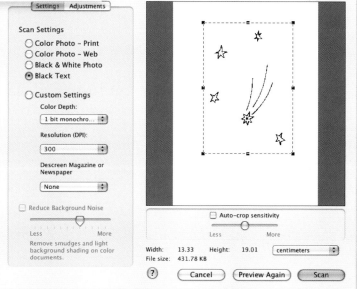

Left Be careful when using "Black and White" settings. Some people refer to grayscale as black and white, and others use the term to mean images made of only pure black and pure white. You will also sometimes see *Black & White Photo* meaning grayscale.

white to make the letter shapes stand out as clearly as possible.

If you want to scan a form or official document so that you can print copies later, pick a high resolution and scan in grayscale or black and white if possible. Don't save this kind of image as a JPEG, because this format will cause visible damage and blurring to what should be crisp text and lines. Saving as a TIFF (compressed or not) or GIF (for grayscale and black and white scans) is a much better choice.

Finally, remember to use the cropping tool when scanning. Don't scan the full area if you just want a small section; preview first to see things properly, then make your selection before continuing on to the *Scan* button. Your scanning software may have an option to do this automatically for you, but check that it has got it right before you go ahead and scan.

You may find that your scanner consistently makes the images it produces a little too dark or light. If so, you can often correct this before you make your scans. It is worth getting the settings right in the first place, because you'll get better, cleaner pictures as a result. The

options you have depend on your scanner's software. Brightness and contrast sliders will be fairly obvious if you have them. Adjusting the white point and black point tells the scanner what it is to regard as the lightest and darkest parts of the image. Start with the standard settings, but if the image needs any overall adjustments, see if you can set these up to happen when you scan rather than afterward.

Above If your image is made up of text or line art consisting of only pure black and pure white, then you should scan it as such (here, it's marked as *Black Text*) to save space.

organizing documents

Keeping track of your files is, of course, a very important thing to do. There's not much point in making the files in the first place if you can't find them when you need them. Make sure you understand the way your computer expects you to organise your documents and then work within those parameters as much as you can. Soon you'll realize that things are where both you and your computer expect them to be, and keeping track of your important files won't be a chore any more.

Whether you use Windows or a Mac, you'll have a place already set up for storing your documents. This is called, sensibly enough, My Documents, or, for Mac users, just Documents, and it is easily found in the navigation panel on the left of Explorer or Finder windows. In here, make folders according to your organizational needs. For example, you

could make one called "House" and keep all house-related items in there, adding subfolders as needed. If you do a lot of work on your computer, you could make a separate folder for each project, or one for each client with further folders in there for the relevant projects.

The My Documents or Documents folder is the most important place for storing most things, but the My Pictures or Pictures folder, although more specialist than the general documents folder, is where your computer expects you to store scans and digital photos that aren't filed in other ways. The same goes for the My Music or Music folder; this is where iTunes will keep your tunes as you digitize your CD collection or buy songs online. In Windows these are both found within the My Documents folder, but on the Mac these are next to it in the user's Home folder.

Below Windows and Mac computers both use similar methods to organize your files. The base of this is usually the "My Documents," or "Documents" folder.

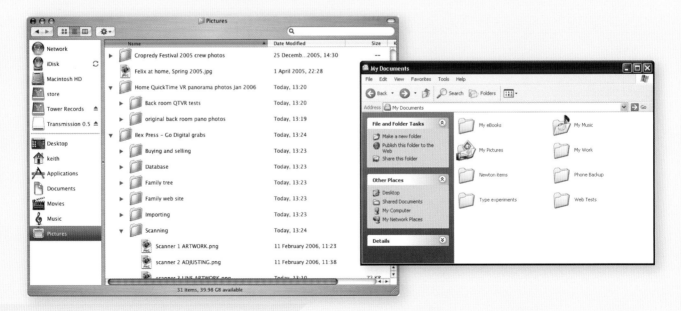

The worst thing you can do is to fall into the habit of saving everything to your Desktop. It is fine for a small number of items, especially if you clear it up regularly, but if left unchecked this will quickly get crowded and hard to sift through.

Naming conventions are a particularly important thing to consider, both for files and for folders. Don't be afraid to be complete; you shouldn't condense a name down into a handful of characters if that won't help you know what the item is at some point in the future. On the flip-side, don't try to fit in a miniature essay about the file or folder. It may help when searching for items, but in most views you won't actually see all that much of a long file name.

When choosing a name for a file, consider who and what it is for. If you'll end up with files called "background" in various different folders, perhaps using a more descriptive name, for example "Smith 2007 calendar project—background photo for January layout" would be much more helpful if you need to sort through files in a hurry. However, this isn't so necessary if the folders the files are in are given descriptive names as well. In this case you could name the outermost folder "Smith 2007 calendar project," make one inside called "January layout"—and call the file in there simply "Background photo."

The only real fly in the ointment comes when making files for use online. Space characters in file and folder names are a bad idea on the Internet, and long, sentence-like names are best avoided too. Replacing spaces with underscores gives a Web-safe simulation, so use those instead.

Below By creating a logical system of folders and subfolders, you'll always be able to keep track of your documents and find them at speed. Modern operating systems have sophisticated search facilities for finding rogue files, but this is no substitute for a well-organized filing system.

importing old files

What if you have old computer files you want to get onto your new computer? How much work this will be depends a lot on how those files are stored right now; are they on a floppy disk of some sort? On the old computer's hard drive? Or perhaps on a removable disk or external disk drive?

The old 3.5" floppy disk used to be a convenient, if very slow and unreliable, way to move small files from one computer to another. These days they've largely been relegated to technology's rubbish heap; if you're a Mac user you won't find a floppy disk drive built into anything made this century, and even PCs are starting to appear without one.

If you absolutely have to get your files from floppy disks and your computer doesn't have the required hardware to read them, you can use an external USB floppy disk drive. Plug it in, insert your disk, and you're ready; the disk will be available in My Computer in your PC or appear on the desktop in your Mac. You may still not be able to read double-density floppy disks (the 800KB kind, not the 1.4MB capacity High Density disks). In this situation you'll have to find an older computer that can transfer your data onto disks you can handle. If your disks are not the standard 3.5" type you'll have to ask yourself quite how important the data they contain really is. Transferring from less common disk types is likely to require specialist help and a corresponding specialist fee to achieve.

If the old computer can connect to the Internet then e-mailing the files to yourself is one simple option, and if they're both networkable then try sharing files on one and accessing them from the other.

Alternatively, burning the work to CD-R makes it easy to get at on new machines and gives you a handy backup at the same time. Finally, you may be able to reuse the old computer's hard disk with your new one, either internally as a second storage device or by getting an external hard disk chassis and installing the drive in that. If you have a lot of data this can often be the simplest, most cost-effective solution.

Getting the old files onto your new computer is only half the battle. You'll then need to be able to read the documents with your modern software. Microsoft Word and most other serious word processors can open the majority of text-based documents, though in some cases you may have a lot of tidying up to do. Obscure database files may be salvageable like this, but you'd be better off—if you can—exporting the data to a common standard such as a tab and return-delimited text file before you move the document to the new computer.

FILE EXTENSIONS

File extensions are useful for identifying the creator application of old files. For example, a file that ends with .txt is recognized as a plain text file that can be opened by NotePad, TextEdit, or something similar. Acrobat PDF files have a .pdf suffix, Microsoft Word documents end in .doc (or .dot for Word template files), JPEG graphics end in .jpg or .jpeg, HTML files end in .htm or .html, and so on.

Most general-purpose graphic files can be dealt with by the software that came with your Mac or PC. The Mac's Preview or Windows' Paint can open up all sorts of files, and Preview acts as a competent PDF viewer as well. Once opened, you can save your old images in whatever newer graphic format you prefer.

Files that come from different computers may not all be named appropriately, and they may even be missing their filename extension. These are additions to the file's name that are used by the operating system to know which program to use when opening the file. Microsoft Windows absolutely requires these suffixes, and they'll be applied to filenames automatically as you make them. Most newer Macintosh programs add these automatically, but these aren't required there and so files may not always have suffixes.

Left Many different disc formats have come and gone over the years. 5 ¼" and 3" disks are no longer in common usage, but some people still use 3.5" disks for transferring small amounts of data. Even the once-ubiquitous Zip discs are no longer very common with the advent of cheap CD-burning equipment.

Left Microsoft Word has a handy feature that enables you to try and recover text from any file. This may mean that you get a lot of junk information along with the text that will have to be trimmed out, but it may be worth it if it's an important file.

Above If there are no external drives available for reading old discs in your modern computer, try connecting your old computer to your new computer over a network and transferring the files directly between them.

All Readable Documents
All Office Documents
All Word Documents
Word Templates
Rich Text Format (RTF)
Text Files
Unicode Text Files
Web Pages
AppleWorks 5 & 6
Microsoft Excel 3.x Worksheet
Microsoft Excel 4.x Worksheet
Microsoft Excel 5.x Worksheet
Microsoft Excel 97–2004 Worksheet
✓ Recover Text from Any File
All Documents

storing information in a database

Whoever you are, and whatever you do, you'll have all sorts of different bits of information to manage. Car insurance details, passport numbers, relatives' birthdays—the list goes on and on. Databases are ideal for managing all this kind of information, but you'll need to decide how deep you want to go before you begin. Regular general-purpose database programs take time to set up, but with planning and practice you can make all sorts of useful information-gathering and sorting tools. Other products are more specialized; address book software, for example, is simply a database program designed for a specific kind of information.

Microsoft Access is the most common database program for Windows users, while for Mac users the most common product is FileMaker Pro, a program that is available in Windows format too. Both of these are flexible, powerful, general-purpose database tools, designed to store largely text-based information and present it again when you browse or search. In contrast, image databases such as iView Media Pro or Extensis Portfolio are meant for managing pictures, movies, sounds, and other media formats. This is a very different kind of task, and is covered in more detail on pages 134–135.

Start off by thinking of a database as a card reference system. Each card is a different record, and you can have all sorts of information stored on each one. You can then search your database to find practically anything you like. Each portion of information is stored as data in a field, whether that's a selection from a drop-down menu, a set of buttons or checkboxes, and so on. You set these up when you first make the database; a text field is good for someone's name, for example, while a pop-up menu with a limited set of choices is probably better for gender or shoe size.

The key to using a database well is careful planning before you start adding the information. Take a good, hard look at the information you want to organize. How does it break down into its individual parts, and are you trying to be too general or too specific? For example, you could set up a family database that tracks a wide range of details for your family and friends, from birthdays and hobbies to favorite foods, allergies, shirt sizes, what you gave them last Christmas, books they've borrowed, and so on. You would probably use a separate database to keep track of things such as product serial numbers, software registration numbers and similar things. Plan it out, thinking hard about the different kinds of information as well as about the different ways you might want to do your searches.

Below Some programs allow you to scan the barcodes on the back of your books, CD cases, and so on, to get information on the type of product it is. This information can then be used to quickly make a database containing details of all of the CDs that you own, for example.

As you can imagine, it is easy to become obsessive about this, trying to capture every last scrap of detail in a database. On the other hand, it really can make retrieving information so much easier than if you have to go rooting through shoeboxes of paperwork.

Getting the data into your computer is the first hurdle. You can type things in, of course, but preferably not if you have a lot to process at once time. OCR software and your scanner will make light work of grabbing large portions of text (see page 121)—but do check the details of the results. It could be frustrating if a vital serial code or phone number was misread when you first put it into the database.

You can use databases for more than just keeping track of serial numbers, and there are various specialized products around. One of the most impressive is Delicious Library. Delicious Library gets around the problem of tedious data entry by using a webcam to read the barcodes from your books and videos. It then grabs the product's details from online databases and adds the product to your own database. Once your library is cataloged, you can browse through the content in all sorts of ways, from flipping through the covers to running text searches; you can synch your library data to your iPod or print a color catalog, and even keep track of who's borrowed things from you.

Below The Delicious Library software doesn't look much like a database at first glance, but really that's all it is—albeit with an extremely well-designed and easy-to-use interface. The software can download images of the products that you log in it, allowing you to browse your virtual bookshelves.

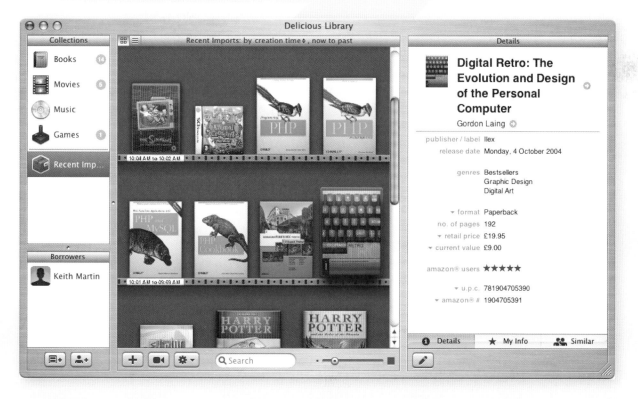

making and using a database

When you make a new database from scratch you'll first have to set up the different fields that will be in each record. Work your way through the list you made when you planned this out (you did make a plan, didn't you?), adding fields and remembering to choose their type as you go. Stick to text, number, date, and time; the other kinds can be tackled once you're more familiar with the product.

Both Access and FileMaker Pro come with ready-made database templates for managing different kinds of information. If what you want to do fits into one of the templates then this will save you some work, but if you want to learn about making

your own database it is worth exploring on your own at least a little. Although there are excellent address books for both the Mac and Windows—including Apple's free Address Book software—by making your own just as an exercise you'll learn a lot about how to make and tailor a database.

In Access, choose *File > New*, then choose *Blank Access Database* and click *OK*. Once you've saved the new database somewhere, you need to create a new table and start adding fields to hold the information. A table is a collection of fields, and an Access database can store one or more tables. Double-click *Create Table in Design View*, then you're ready to make the various fields, or columns as they will be viewed to start with.

In FileMaker Pro, choose *File > New Database* (if the *New Database* window isn't already open), click *Create a New Empty File*, and click *OK*. Once you've named and saved the new database somewhere you'll be taken straight to the process of adding new fields.

Start with a field called "Name," then a field called "Birthday"—make this one a *Date* (or *Date/Time*) field. Add a field called "Address," one called "Phone," and another called "E-mail," and you're done. In Access, when you save you'll be asked to define a field as a "primary key," something that's useful when working across multiple tables. You don't need to define one here. Now that you have your database set up the next step is to start adding your information to it.

Access users will see a spreadsheet-like display. To enter some data, switch to the "Datasheet" view by clicking the button in the top-left of the Access

Below Database software such as FileMaker Pro enables you to create databases for your information with the minimum of fuss. It can take a while to familiarize yourself with the interface at first, though.

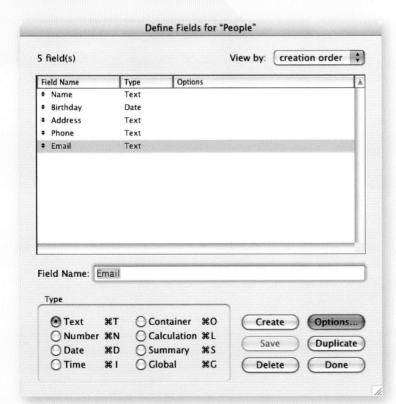

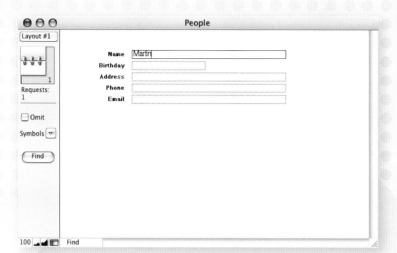

Left Once you've
defined your fields
in FileMaker Pro,
you can go ahead
and add the required
information into them.

Left With all of the
information entered,
your database is
ready for searching.
Databases are
extremely powerful
search tools because
of the way that the
data within them is
structured, and a lot
of this is down to the
fields that you create
in the first place, so
make sure you plan
your fields in advance.

window. Click and start typing your data,
dropping down to a new line to make a
new record as you go.

FileMaker presents the new database in
"Form" view, ready for data entry, so start
typing. Choose *Records > New Record* to
make a new record, and use the navigation
panel on the left to go back and forth.
Choose *View > View as Table* to see your
database records in a spreadsheet-style view
instead. This packs more onto your screen,
although it can be rather overwhelming.

Now that you've added information
it's time to try some searches. The basic
method for searching is the same in
FileMaker and Access. FileMaker users
should choose *View > Find Mode* to put
the current form into the *Find* mode,
whereas Access users should first click in
the field they're going to use for the search
and then choose *Edit > Find*. Type what
you're looking for and press Enter (or click
FileMaker's *Find* button), and you're shown
the records that match your search.

making and using a database continued

Right Once all of the fields are set up in your database, you can choose various ways of displaying the data. Some programs even include special views such as *Envelope*, that displays your address data in a form that's ready for printing onto address labels or directly onto envelopes.

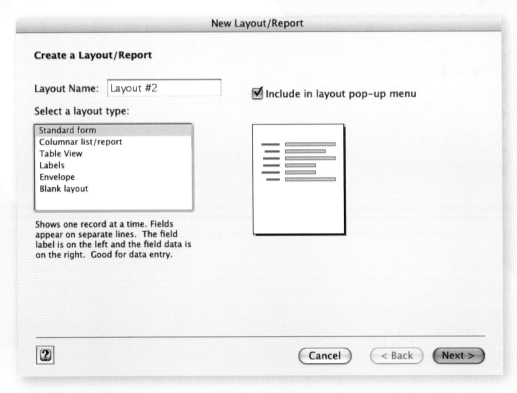

New Layout/Report

Create a Layout/Report

Layout Name: Layout #2

☑ Include in layout pop-up menu

Select a layout type:

Standard form
Columnar list/report
Table View
Labels
Envelope
Blank layout

Shows one record at a time. Fields appear on separate lines. The field label is on the left and the field data is on the right. Good for data entry.

Cancel   < Back   Next >

Tailoring a database

Remember, the database you've made and populated with your information holds all your data—but it doesn't have to show it all in a single layout. Design different views for different uses and switch between them at will. Right now the spreadsheet display in Access and even FileMaker's layout view are pretty basic. To tailor FileMaker's form layout to fit more into certain fields, the "Address" field for example, choose *View > Layout Mode*. Now you can arrange and scale each field, add blocks of color, change text settings, and generally make this into a more usefully arranged form.

To make a form to display your Access information in a more controlled manner, click the *Forms* button on the left of the screen, then double-click *Create Form Using Wizard*. Next, select the fields you want in the form view (choose all of them), click *Next*, select a layout, then a style, then name it and choose to open the form. Once finished you'll see your form. To change the layout, click the *Design* button in the top left of the window and alter things as you like.

When your database has a decent amount of data stored away you'll find that you want different kinds of information at different times; maybe an overview of all the records that match a general search for birthdays one time and a detailed list of the result for a more specific search the next. You can make different layouts to show your

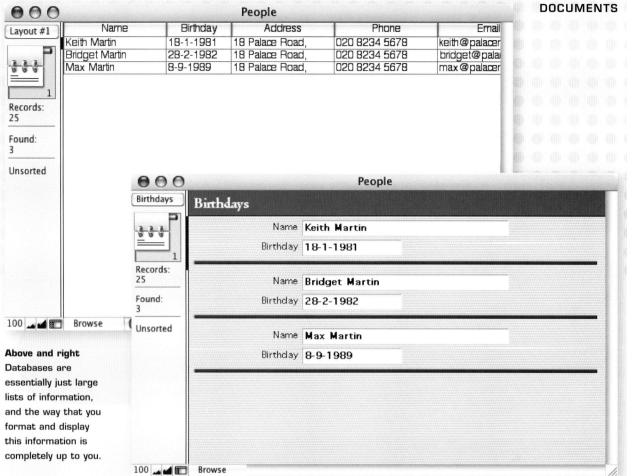

Above and right
Databases are essentially just large lists of information, and the way that you format and display this information is completely up to you.

data in different ways. Remember, the information you've collected is entirely separate from the way you present it. You can make a new layout showing just some of the data fields and with different items highlighted, shown in a bolder, larger typeface, or employ any other layout trick you can think of for helping you see your information the way you want.

In Access, simply repeat the process used to create a form, but choose just the fields you want in this layout before finishing this step. With FileMaker Pro, choose *View > Layout Mode*, then choose *Layouts > New Layout/Report* to open the *New Layout/Report* window. From here, pick the first, the *Standard Form*, to get a new layout with all fields shown.

You can delete individual fields from your database layout—remember, deleting fields doesn't remove the actual data from the database, just the field from the layout—and then format the remaining ones as required. You may find it handy to have a layout which is created specifically for data entry, something that places all the fields in a logical, compact arrangement, and to then use other layouts for browsing and searching.

Don't spend too long trying to reinvent the wheel; basic data management tasks can be satisfied very well with existing free or cheap readymade programs. But if you want to organise a slightly less ordinary collection of facts and figures, this is the way to do it.

image archives

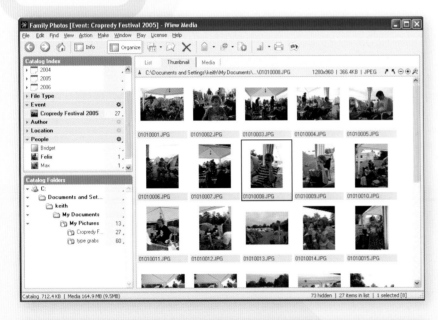

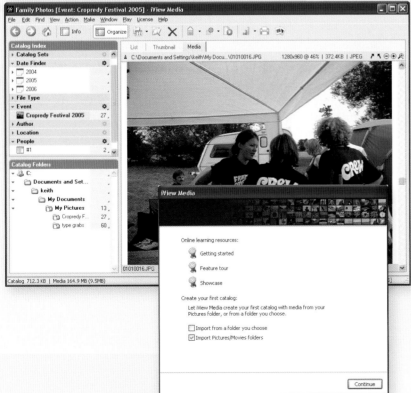

When it comes to storing and keeping track of images, a regular database program is a poor choice. Those are well-tuned for handling text data, and they store everything within the database document itself. But when it comes to pictures you need something that works in a different way. Fortunately, there are a number of excellent image-oriented database products available that can help you handle all your digital photos, scans, and more. Both iView Media and Extensis Portfolio are more than ready to track many thousands of images and help you find your photos quickly. They both work in similar ways, and they can track and organize sounds and videos as well. Extensis Portfolio and the Pro version of iView Media are equally adept at cataloging and sorting many other kinds of files including page layout documents, fonts, and word processor and spreadsheet files.

Of course, these features go way past what's needed in an image archive tool, but if you want a very flexible alternative to the normal Windows Explorer or Macintosh Finder methods of managing your documents, these products can be a great help. When you've found the picture you want to use, you can open it in another program from there or even just drag and drop it into a page layout.

Left and above
iView Media is a very easy-to-use program for cataloging your images. It allows you to view your pictures in three main views—*List*, *Thumbnail*, and *Media*. List gives a simple text list of all of the images for easy searching, Thumbnail gives thumbnail images for browsing, and Media gives a detailed view of single images.

There are numerous other products around, from the ultra-basic to the slick and fully-featured. Mac users should look first at Apple's iPhoto that comes with new Macs as standard and as part of the iLife software suite. This only works with images and video clips; it won't catalog other kinds of documents, but it does provide "photo albums" for grouping images in different sets and basic keyword tagging and searching to help track down items. It also offers extensive publishing options, from printing cards and ordering bound albums to Web photo galleries and sending by e-mail.

Windows users can start by looking at the photo-oriented Lightbox or, for handling many other kinds of files as well, Image Works. Image Works is designed to provide many of the features found in Portfolio and iView Media, including slide shows, Web photo galleries, batch-conversions, and catalogs of removable media such as CDs.

Once you've chosen your image archive tool you'll have to set it up, add your pictures to it, and make sure keywords are added to the appropriate items. These things can make it much easier to manage large collections of images, but only if you start out properly. Fortunately, it isn't hard at all to get started with a product such as iView Media.

When it is launched, you can make a new "media catalog" from your Pictures and Movies folders. The media is imported and presented in the catalog window, with tabs for showing the items in detailed list view, an array of thumbnails, or in close-up "media" form. An *Info* panel shows exhaustive details about selected items, a *Caption* panel lets you add information

to them, and an *Organize* panel lets you tag and filter items by date, event, author, location, people, and other keywords. To add a keyword to the *People* list, click *Organize*, then click *People*. Now click the cogwheel icon in the *People* bar, choose *Add*, and type a person's name. Finally, drag an image onto the new name. Now when you click that name you'll see just the items that have been linked to it. You can add many different keywords, so it makes sense to tag your photos and movies with all the different names of the people in the shots.

Once you've found the items you want, you can open or move the images themselves, create a photo gallery for your website, run a slide show, or make a printed version of your media catalog. If you have files on a CD you can include these too; the catalog remembers where the originals are and lets you browse the database for media even if the disc isn't in your computer.

Below iPhoto enables you to add keywords—called tags—to your photos. For example, you could search for all images with the tag "vacation 2006."

section five
communication

e-mail

E-mail is a big part of many people's lives, but most still don't know how to use it effectively. Start by getting to know the e-mail software you use. Macintosh users have Apple's Mail program installed as standard. This is an excellent e-mail program with some very useful features such as thread highlighting; select a message and all related ones will be picked out as well. Windows users can choose Microsoft's Outlook Express or the more comprehensive Outlook, part of the Office software suite and possibly the most widely used e-mail tool around. Alternatively, both Mac and Windows users can choose from a large number of different programs such as Thunderbird and Eudora, both of which are far more secure against Windows e-mail viruses than Outlook Express.

Setting up an e-mail program can be a daunting task if you've never done it before. Fortunately, whatever program you use will prompt you for details as you start, so you just have to know a few key pieces of information. These are your e-mail address, whether your mail account is POP or IMAP (or .Mac if you're using Apple's Mail), the incoming mail server address (for example mail.mydomain.com) and the outgoing server address (for example smtp.mydomain.com), and your e-mail account's username and password. The outgoing server address may be the same as the incoming one, but don't assume this.

When your e-mail program picks up your mail it first contacts the mail server

Above Just as with any other, it's a good idea to set up a system for storing your e-mail messages rather than letting them pile up in your Inbox. All e-mail programs allow you to set up folders for this.

Right You will find—especially if you give out your e-mail freely on the Web—that you will receive a lot of junk, or "spam," mail. Many e-mail programs have filters for removing spam.

computer, gives it your username and password, then proceeds to retrieve any waiting e-mails. It goes through a similar process when sending e-mail, too.

Your e-mail software will normally be set up to check for new mail automatically every now and then, as long as it can tell that you're online. If you want to check manually there will be a *Check* or *Send and Receive* button to click. The *Compose* or *New* button will create a new message; type an e-mail address (these always have an @ symbol and no spaces), enter your message, and click *Queue* or *Send.* Queued e-mails will be sent when you next receive your mail, but you may also have to click a *Send* button to do this.

There's a certain etiquette involved in writing an e-mail, but don't believe anyone who claims that there's just one right way to do this. As you'd expect, the right way to construct an e-mail depends a lot on who you're talking to. They are less formally structured than written letters—you're expected to get to the point rather than including traditional preambles—but just remember to apply a little common sense. As you'd expect, messages to company departments shouldn't be all that chatty, whereas a quick note to a friend is the equivalent to you just popping your head around a corner.

E-mail mailing lists are a very important part of using the Internet to your advantage, and these can become fairly social, close-knit virtual communities. Take a little time once you join a list to read its archives and get a feel for the way its members talk to each other. When you do send a message or a reply to a mailing list always remember that you're speaking to absolutely everyone

> **KEY E-MAIL DETAILS**
>
> **Your e-mail address**
> i.e. you@somewhere.co.uk
>
> **E-mail account type**
> **POP or IMAP**
>
> **Incoming server address**
> i.e. mail.somewhere.co.uk
>
> **Outgoing server address**
> i.e. smtp.somewhere.co.uk
>
> **Username**
> i.e. digital123
>
> **Password**
> **Keep this safe and secret**

else that's joined the list; your e-mail goes to the list server and is then bounced out to every other member automatically. If you wouldn't say what you're about to post to the whole crowd then post it to an individual instead, or don't say it at all. When replying you should also take care to trim down the "quoted" content of the message. It is helpful to leave enough there to give others a bit of context for your reply, but that's all that's needed. Finally, basic "me too" replies generally do very little other than clogging up everyone's incoming mail; expand on your comment in some way or bite your tongue!

If someone annoys you it is all too easy to fire off a vitriolic reply in a few seconds. The trouble is, once it is sent there's no way to unsend it, and mere minutes later you may regret what you just wrote. Such angry e-mails are often called "flames." Don't respond to these, if you ignore the people who wrote them, they will usually leave.

skype and Internet phone calls

With a computer and a broadband connection you can go digital with your phone calls and speak to family, friends, and colleagues around the world for free. Voice over IP, or VoIP for short—the acronym is pronounced as a word—is the latest revolution thundering along on the back of the Internet.

There are a number of different VoIP products on the market, but the best-known and easiest to use with your computer is Skype. This is a free software-only product available from www.skype.com, and it lets users make calls to other Skype users anywhere in the world for nothing. Better still, you're not limited to talking to Skype users; with a system named SkypeOut you can call any landline phone anywhere and pay local call rates. Simply download and install Skype, pick a username when you first run it, and you're done. To add someone to your contacts list choose *Contacts > Add a Contact* and type their Skype username. If you don't know that, choose *Contacts > Search for People* and look them up.

Okay, you may need to get yourself a little more sorted out first: you'll need some kind of speakers and microphone in order to speak to someone and hear their replies. All computers should have speakers and many laptops come with microphones built in, but you'll be better off buying something meant specifically for this task instead. You have two options; either a headset and microphone combination such as the Sennheiser M145, or a regular-looking phone that connects to your computer via USB, such as the VoIPVoice Cyberphone K. You'll have to hold one of these to your ear like a real phone, but

most USB phone handsets have their own ringer and you're less likely to trip over the wires when you have an unexpected incoming call. Do check for compatibility first; not all USB phones work with Skype or even fully with the Mac.

Skype offers two services you can add to your regular Skype account; SkypeOut and SkypeIn. SkypeOut allows you to call regular phones in many parts of the world for a local call rate, and other places, even cell phones, for not much more. You'll need to log onto the Skype site and buy some SkypeOut credit in advance, but once done you can make calls to any number you like, economically.

SkypeIn is the flip side of calling non-Skype users; it lets non-Skype users call you on your Skype phone. For a small fee you can have a regular phone number that connects straight to the Skype setup on your computer. You can even pick the country you want the number to be in, so you can live in the UK but have a phone number in the US, Hong Kong, Brazil, or one of a number of other countries. Anyone living near your number pays local call rates to speak to you on that number. Better still, you get voicemail along with the number, so people can leave messages if your computer happens to be turned off when they call.

Keep your eye on other VoIP products, as this is an area that is going to expand and mature quickly. But for now, Skype is easy and flexible, and it has a lot to offer.

Video calling is the next stage on from voice, and this is something that's been tackled already with some other online communications software. Apple's iChat and some other AIM-compatible instant

Left Skype keeps track of the duration of the call and displays it prominently on the screen. This is especially important if you are using the SkypeOut service, so you can see how much money you are spending. Rather than charge the call directly to your credit card, you buy credit from Skype in advance and use that to pay. Remember that this is only for Skype's extra services, the basic computer-to-computer calling service is completely free.

message text "chat" tools have expanded to include voice and video chat as well, using regular USB or FireWire Web cams to capture the video feed. As long as you're using a compatible chat client program, the end result is the same as

Skype and other VoIP products, but you can't use them to make calls to and from telephones. With the next version of its software, Skype is moving toward video calls as well, so you may want to add a webcam to the shopping list too.

Above Skype keeps track of your contacts' status, so you can see who's online. You can set your status to say you're busy or away from the computer.

making a weblog (blog)

Whether you're the diary-writing type who enjoys putting down your every thought, you want to publish a regular news bulletin, or you simply want to keep a journal during a particular event, weblogs—normally known by the more familiar name "blogs"—are a superb solution, and they're easier to make than many people realize. Some methods of making blogs even allow for others to contribute comments to the articles you make, so this can be a very handy way for far-flung family members to keep each other informed of what's happening.

Below Blogging sounds like a complex, arcane artform, but in reality it's very simple to start up your own blog.

Below The easiest way to set up a blog is by using Blogger. This uses templates to minimize the layout work you have to do.

Left Once you've chosen your template and entered a few start-up details, you're ready to begin blogging. Be warned: it can turn into a very addictive hobby!

Blogs are hosted on websites, and the information you type into a blog entry can normally be seen both in the form of a page in your favorite Web browser or by using a special RSS reader. RSS is the name for the way blog articles are formatted, organized and delivered. It stands for Rich Site Summary, Really Simple Syndication, and also RDF Site Summary, depending on which variation you're using, but don't be put off; all good blog software or services will take care of this for you. When people subscribe to your blog using their chosen blog reader software they'll get your new journal entries automatically; they don't even have to remember to check a website.

The easiest way to get yourself a blog is to sign up with a blogging service. There are a large number available, but Blogger is both popular and free, and it offers a decent selection of template designs for your blog's page layout.

To begin, go to www.blogger.com and click the *Create Your Blog Now* link. Pick a username and password, give your blog a title, pick a "blogspot.com" address, then choose a template from the list of options. That's it; now click the *Start Posting* link and add your first entry. Give it a title and just start typing, then click *Publish Post* when you're happy. Your blog address will be the one you selected earlier, for example "justgodigital.blogspot.com."

You can choose to add a description of your blog, add it to Blogger's directory of hosted blogs, allow visitors to post comments about what you've said, and much more. Allowing comments, which is turned on by default, can make your blog a very interactive, collaborative thing. You can

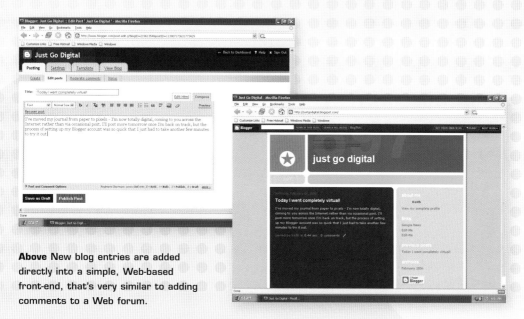

Above New blog entries are added directly into a simple, Web-based front-end, that's very similar to adding comments to a Web forum.

Left Once you've written your entry, click the *Publish Post* button and your entry will be styled and added to your blog.

let anyone do this, restrict it to registered Blogger members, or only those who you add as a team member of your blog.

Another way to run your own blog is to use software on your own computer to create the files and have those uploaded somewhere for others to read. The Macintosh-only iWeb, from Apple, does this well, although you'll need a ".Mac" subscription too. RapidWeaver, from www.realmacsoftware.com, also includes similar blog creation features.

With iWeb, you work on your own computer and add blog entries as new pages, then you "publish" the new articles to your site when you're done. By using iWeb you can mix Web pages with blog pages, include "podcasts" (audio blogs you record yourself), and even video-based content. The only real downside is that you can't add blog entries when you're not in front of your computer. So, if you want to post a day-by-day account of your big holiday, for example, you'd better remember to take a laptop with you.

Open iWeb, click the *Plus* icon in the bottom-left corner, then pick a theme and the blog page type. This opens a templated layout where you can add (or delete) a photo and type in your journal title, date, and content and you can play with the layout all you like. This is automatically stored as a blog on your .Mac account when you publish it. When you add a new blog page any previous articles can be found in the *Blog Archive* page that iWeb makes for you.

Below iWeb is Apple's addition to the blogging market. Along with its ease of use, one of the main benefits of iWeb is that you can add podcasts to your blog.

producing a family website

Have you ever wanted a website but didn't know where to start or who to ask? Fear not, it can actually be easy and fun—as long as you make the right choices. Web design is normally considered to be a complex, technically demanding task. At some levels it can be, but for most kinds of Web page there are now tools that do virtually all of the hard work for you—leaving you free to get your information out there on the Web. All you need is the right software and some simple Web hosting, which you may already have as part of your Internet access provider's connection deal. If you need to find a company to host your website you'll soon realize that there are almost too many to count. You're not even limited to your own country; it doesn't matter where they are in the world, on the Internet they're only a click away. Of course, if you ever need telephone advice you'd probably be better off if you're in the same general time zone. 24-hour phone support isn't unheard of, but long-distance calls can be expensive unless you use an Internet-based phone service such as Skype (see pages 140–141).

With most traditional Web production software you'll need to prepare everything before starting to assemble your pages. A few programs will do this for you too, performing tasks such as turning your digital snaps into Web-ready images as you work. This is by far the nicest and most pleasant approach, so take advantage of this if your software provides this feature.

On the Macintosh, there are some very good website creation applications around. Apple's iWeb is very easy to use, although you'll need a .Mac account from Apple to make the most of it. Alternatively, there's

RapidWeaver, which is good for putting your words and pictures into ready-made templates, or Freeway Express, which is ideal for making your own free-form layouts.

With RapidWeaver and iWeb you simply add a new page to your site window and choose what kind it is to be—photo gallery, newsletter, blog, and so on—from a list. Photo galleries take their contents from your iPhoto library, and all the design work is done for you by the templates. These are very well-designed, but in RapidWeaver you have no real say over their appearance. You get more design control with iWeb, but it is less flexible if you want to make more than one site or host it somewhere other than a .Mac account. For full design and uploading freedom, but fewer ready-made templates, try Freeway Express. It guides you less but lets you design far more freely, and, like iWeb, it takes care of making images Web-friendly as well as generating the Web page code for you.

Windows users will find Web Page Maker an easy and inexpensive tool for assembling page designs, although you will need to prepare your images for the Web before you add them to your pages. Another product worth trying is Nvu. This is more of a traditional Web authoring tool with acceptable layout controls and full access to the HTML code if you want it.

Getting started with a program such as Nvu isn't particularly hard, although you should prepare your images as JPEGs or GIFs first. Once you're ready to start assembling, open an Nvu page, choose *Insert > Image*, and pick a graphic. To make the item a layer so you can reposition it, click the *Layer* button next to the *Font* drop-down menu and drag

the item by its crosshair handle. Choose *Insert > Table* and make a simple one-cell table, type something into it, and turn it into a layer. You can use this as a simple repositionable text box for your page design. Save your page, then choose *File > Publish* and enter your website's FTP details to upload it to your website.

Getting started with Freeway on the Mac is more like ordinary page layout. Start with a template for simplicity, then drag any image from iPhoto or the Finder into the page, then move it to where you want it and crop it by dragging the box handles. The graphic will be made into a Web-safe JPEG or GIF for you when you publish. Click the *Graphic* button and draw out a new box, then click inside it and type to make graphic headlines. For regular paragraphs of text, Click the *HTML* button and draw out an HTML box on your page, then click inside it and type or paste your text. Use the *Inspector* palette to control formatting, fine-tune its position, and so on. Choose *Upload* and use your website's FTP settings to publish your designs to your website.

Whatever software you use, when you've finished your pages you must upload your work for others to see it. This is fairly simple using the *Publish* or *Upload* feature of your website software and the FTP connection details of your website.

Images on your Web pages must be the right format or your visitors won't be able to see them properly. If your website software doesn't do this for you, you'll need to open and save your graphics and photos in the right way before putting them into your page layouts. The two most widely supported image formats on the Web are GIF and JPEG. It is pretty simple to know

which one to use: the GIF format is best used for graphics that have lots of crisp, sharp edges and flat colors, while the JPEG format is best used for softer, more photographic subjects.

You can use Paint, or Preview on the Mac, to open and export your graphics and photos as JPEGs and GIFs, but Paint's editing features are very crude and Preview's are effectively nonexistent. For any serious image editing or correction work, you should use something like Adobe Photoshop Elements. This software also contains a simple *Save For Web* feature for correctly preparing your images.

When you're putting your pages together don't forget to consider how things will feel to a visitor. For example, text on a dark or busy background can be surprisingly difficult to read, and if you put dozens of pictures on one page people will have to wait longer for that page to finish loading when they visit.

Above Although there's a lot to be said for using a standard design to make your site easier for visitors to navigate through, have fun experimenting a little bit. Remember that websites don't need to look like websites—with a few scans of paper, you can make your site look like your desktop.

using FTP

FTP stands for File Transfer Protocol. You're only likely to use an FTP program if you want to work on your own website, but if you do that, FTP is the primary way to upload the various files that go to make up your Web pages.

Most Web design programs include FTP uploading features right in the application, so you can design your page then tell the layout software to upload it for you. But if you ever needed to clear out old, outdated files from your site or upload something separately, then you'll need a proper FTP "client" program. Despite sounding like things only meant for advanced users, modern FTP client software is generally very easy to use. To make an FTP connection, first you'll need to know the address of the FTP server, normally something like ftp.MySite.com but sometimes a numeric "IP" address such as 123.234.345.456. You will also need your FTP username and password. Finally, you may need to know the "path" to the right part of the FTP server; this is the route from the top level of where you log in down into the right folder for your website. You may not be given one, which means either you don't need one or you'll need to spot the folder and double-click it to get inside. In these cases the folder name you're looking for is likely to be something like "web," "www," "htdocs," or possibly your website's domain name.

There are many FTP client programs to choose from. Windows users should try CuteFTP, while Windows and Macintosh users alike can use CuteFTP Pro. On the Mac-specific front, Transmit and Captain FTP are two FTP programs that are certainly worth considering. These all work in essentially the same simple way; connect, and you're shown the files and folders on the FTP server. From here you can either drag and drop files from the website to download to your computer, or from your computer to upload to the website. You can also perform maintenance tasks, such as deleting files by selecting them and clicking Delete. Finally, you can store your FTP connection details to make it easy to reconnect again.

Below Once you have entered the required details into your FTP program, it should remember them all for you, meaning that you don't need to type them in every time.

Left Some FTP applications will offer tips when you start them up. It's worth reading these through when you're learning the application, but after that you can turn them off.

Automated transfers, sometimes called synchronised or mirrored folders, mean that all you have to do to maintain your remote files is move things in and out of your synchronised local one. Choose a folder on your computer, choose the folder (also known as directory) on the remote FTP server to link it to, then just move things in and out of that folder. Your FTP software needs to be running to do this of course, but it will keep things in synch automatically.

Files and folders stored on an FTP server generally shouldn't have spaces in their names, certainly not if the files are meant for use in Web pages. For non-Web files and for programs, it is generally a good idea to encode them into Zip or StuffIt archives before uploading them to an FTP server. As well as making sure that everything copies across without losing subtle settings, it also helps to keep file sizes down. And this makes the uploading and downloading process faster.

KEY FTP DETAILS

FTP server address
i.e. ftp.somewhere.co.uk or
123.234.345.456

Username
i.e. digital123

Password
Keep this safe and secret

Path
i.e. files/web/

Above and left Most FTP applications give you two windows on the screen. This enables you to set one to a folder on your hard drive and one to a folder on your website so you can quickly drag and drop files between them. You can also set these to two separate website folders if desired.

buying and selling on the Internet

Internet shopping is now huge business. From books and groceries to holidays, cars, computers, and music, there's little you can't buy online. Buying goods online is safer than many people think as long as you're sensible. You'll usually pay using a credit or debit card or with an Internet payment service such as PayPal. PayPal is a popular way to pay for goods and services on eBay and many other sites across the Internet. This service acts as a payment broker, almost a bank. When you pay for something using PayPal the money comes from your account, topped up automatically by your credit card if necessary. Setting up an account can take a little time, but it does help simplify online purchasing in many Web stores.

However you pay, the most important point is to stay secure. If you're paying using a credit or debit card you should be sure the payment page is secure, one that transmits your details in encrypted form. Your Web browser will show a padlock icon in its window (not just in the page itself) and the address will begin with https:// rather than just http://—the "s" indicates a secure connection. Paying using PayPal will involve stepping across to the PayPal site, logging into your secure account pages and confirming the payment. Once you've finished, keep a record of what you've bought, where you bought it and when. Know how long delivery is going to be and contact the seller if there's a delay.

eBay is one of the biggest names when it comes to selling online. This is a virtual marketplace where anyone can come along, register, and offer things up for auction. eBay provides the venue, and people come along and use it to sell virtually anything at all to whoever will pay. Although there are rules for buyers and sellers, eBay has no direct control over what's sold. In effect, the whole of eBay runs on trust. It is quite possible for someone to take your money and send you some junk or nothing at all in return—but in fact, most people want to keep on using eBay, and they know they'd get negative feedback from their buyers or be kicked off eBay if they tried to pull a fast one. The same thing discourages bidders from backing out after winning an auction. Good feedback is the key to confidence for both buyers and sellers and a key part of eBay's functioning, and it works pretty well almost all of the time.

Left and below You've probably heard many horror stories about buying items on the Internet. Although you do have to be wary, most of these stories are completely overblown. Buying on the Internet is generally as safe as doing so in a mall.

Searching eBay for goods is simple enough. You can browse idly through the many different areas to see what's around, but for serious shopping you should use its search features. Imagine the kinds of words a seller might choose for their auction and use those in your search. If you find something you're interested in but you're not ready to bid for just yet, you can add it to a watch list. This helps you get back to them quickly if you want to make comparisons or go ahead and bid. The advanced search lets you view completed listings instead of current auctions so you can get a feel for how much different things tend to sell for.

You should have a mental checklist that you always go through before you go ahead and bid on anything. Does the seller have good feedback? What payment methods are listed? Where is the seller based and how much is the postage? What about the auction description—is it complete and informative? Is the item really what you think it is? Don't be put off entirely by limited descriptions, but do be wary. Ask the seller questions before you bid, not after.

You'll need to guard yourself against auction fever. It is all too easy to get carried away when bidding against others and ending up paying more than you should. You should always decide what's the most you're willing to pay, and remember to factor the postage costs into this figure. When you make a bid the maximum price that you submit won't necessarily be what you'll have to pay; the actual price gets raised bid by bid, with earlier bids taking precedence in case of matching amounts. When an auction nears its end there can be a small flurry

Above eBay is an online marketplace where you can buy or sell virtually anything. It's a great place to find bargains, but beware of getting carried away and buying hundreds of things that you don't need.

of activity as people try to grab a bargain, and this is where the danger of auction fever is at its greatest. Be ready to walk away from something if the price gets a bit steep. If you win, contact the seller and pay up as soon as possible.

When you want to sell something, remember your eBay buying experiences and do your best to make an auction that will attract buyers. Use a digital camera to take photos of the item—even snaps from a cell phone camera are better than nothing—then click on eBay's *Sell* link and walk through the auction creation steps. Finally, when your item is sold, send it off as soon as you've been paid—and never forget to leave feedback whether you're buying or selling.

Above PayPal is a secure service for money transactions. Once you have an account with them, you can use it to pay for many items online without having to keep giving out your credit card details.

section six
reference

useful Web addresses

PHOTOGRAPHS

SOFTWARE

Adobe Photoshop Elements – www.adobe.com

Corel Paint Shop Pro – www.corel.com

FotoFinish Studio – www.fotofinish.com

Ulead PhotoImpact – www.ulead.com

Digital Image Suite – www.microsoft.com/products/imaging

PhotoStudio – www.arcsoft.com

PhotoPlus – www.serif.com/photoplus

PhotoSuite – www.roxio.com/en/products/photosuite

PhotoLightning – www.photolightning.com

SCANNERS

Canon – www.canon.com

Epson – www.epson.com

Hewlett-Packard – www.hp.com

Microtek – www.microtek.com

ONLINE PRINTERS

Kodak EasyShare – www.kodakgallery.com

Sony ImageStation – www.imagestation.com

Printroom.com – www.printroom.com

Fujifilm – www.fujifilm.net

PhotoBox – www.photobox.co.uk

Bonusprint – www.bonusprint.com

Club Photo – www.clubphoto.com

Ezprints – www.ezprints.com

Fotki – www.fotki.com

Funtigo – www.funtigo.com

ImageEvent – www.imageevent.com

PhotoShow – www.ourpictures.com

Phanfare – www.phanfare.com

Photosite – www.photosite.com

PhotoWorks – www.photoworks.com

PictureTrail – www.picturetrail.com

Pixagogo – www.pixagogo.com

Shutterfly – www.shutterfly.com

VIDEO

EDITING AND AUTHORING SOFTWARE

Movie Maker – www.microsoft.com/windowsxp/moviemaker

iMovie – http://www.apple.com/ilife/imovie

iDVD – http://www.apple.com/ilife/idvd

Pinnacle Studio – www.pinnaclesys.com

Audition – www.adobe.com

Premiere Elements – www.adobe.com

ShowBiz – www.arcsoft.com

AutoProducer – ww.muvee.com

PowerDirector – www.cyberlink.com

PowerProducer – www.cyberlink.com

VideoWave – www.roxio.com

Vegas Movie Studio – www.sonymediasoftware.com

VideoStudio – www.ulead.com

WinDVD Creator – www.intervideo.com

DVD MovieFactory – www.ulead.com

MyDVD – www.sonic.com

TELECINE TRANSFER

DVD-tek – www.dvd-tek.com

Pennylane Video – www.videoencoding.biz

EverMediia – www.evermedia.co.uk

Transfer Video – www.transfervideo.com

Film to Video – www.film-to-video.com

Home Movie.com – www.homemovie.com

Home Movie Depot – www.homemoviedepot.com

MUSIC

EDITING AND ENCODING SOFTWARE
Audacity – http://audacity.sourceforge.net
Audition – www.adobe.com/products/audition
CDex – http://cd-to-mp3.audiolaunch.com/cd-ripper
Audion – www.panic.com/audion

MUSIC MANAGEMENT SOFTWARE
iTunes – www.apple.com/itunes
Media Player – www.microsoft.com/windows/windowsmedia
Winamp – www.winamp.com
Audionaut Music Manager – www.audionaut.com/software
Helium Music Manager – http://helium-music-manager.com

COMPRESSION TECHNOLOGIES
Fraunhofer IIS – http://www.iis.fraunhofer.de
LAME – http://lame.sourceforge.net
MP3pro – http://www.codingtechnologies.com

ONLINE MUSIC STORES
iTunes – accessed through the iTunes application
Connect – www.connect.com
Napster – www.napster.com
MP3.com – www.mp3.com
Insound – www.insound.com
Karma Download.com – www.karmadownload.com

STREAMING RADIO STATIONS
National Public Radio – www.npr.org
BBC Radio – www.bbc.co.uk/radio
Canadian Broadcasting Corporation – www.cbc.ca/listen
RealPlayer – www.real.com
Resonance FM – www.resonancefm.com
Club 977 – www.club977.com
Club 977 Hitz – www.club977hitz.com
Club 977 Country – www.totalcountry.net
Sky.FM – www.sky.fm
SHOUTcast – www.shoutcast.com

DOCUMENTS

OCR SOFTWARE
TextBridge and OmniPage – www.nuance.com
Readiris Pro – www.irislink.com
FineReader – www.abbyy.com

DATABASE SOFTWARE
Delicious Library – www.delicious-monster.com
Access – http://office.microsoft.com
FileMaker Pro – www.filemaker.com

IMAGE CATALOGING SOFTWARE
iView Media – www.iview-multimedia.com
Extensis Portfolio – www.extensis.com
iLife – www.apple.com/ilife
Lightbox – www.luminosity.co.uk
Image Works – www.offsitelabs.com

COMMUNICATION

E-MAIL SOFTWARE
Thunderbird – www.mozilla.com/thunderbird
Eudora – www.eudora.com

VOIP SOFTWARE
Skype – www.skype.com

FTP SOFTWARE
CuteFTP – www.cuteftp.com
Transmit – www.panic.com
Captain FTP – captainftp.xdsnet.de

WEB PAGE CREATION SOFTWARE
RapidWeaver – www.realmacsoftware.com
FreeWay Express – www.softpress.com
Web Page Maker – www.webpage-maker.com
Nvu – www.nvu.com

PHOTOGRAPHS GLOSSARY

CCD

Charge-Coupled Device. The light sensor that digital cameras use to capture images. Essentially, a grid of red-, green-, and blue-sensitive elements whose data is combined to make up an image.

Digital Camera

Like the traditional film camera, a digital cameras goes through the same process of opening a shutter to enable light to pass through the lens, but instead of the light hitting photo-sensitive film, it instead hits the CCD. This device records the image and saves it onto a memory card ready to be transferred onto a computer.

DPI

Dots Per Inch. Inkjet printer resolution is defined in terms of DPI. It is the number of dots of ink that the printer can fit into an inch of paper. The greater the DPI, the better quality the image.

Feather

A term used for the softened edge of a selection. Feathering is used to create better blends between elements in digital photomontages. Without feathering, selections have hard, and highly visible edges.

FireWire

Also known as i.Link or IEEE 1394. FireWire is a high-speed format used for connecting devices to computers. It is most commonly found on digital video devices, though some high-end cameras also contain this connection.

Marching Ants

A dotted line used by digital photoediting applications to denote a selection. The dotted line is usually animated, giving it the appearance of marching ants.

Memory Card

The storage format used by digital cameras. There are many types of memory card available, such as SD, Compact Flash, Mem Stick, Microdrive, and so on, so be sure to check which type your camera uses before buying new cards.

Photoshop Elements

One of the most common digital photo-editing applications. Elements began life as a cut-down version of its parent application, Photoshop, but has since grown into a more focused application for amateur photographers.

Pixel

The smallest unit of a digital image. A pixel is a single-colored dot displayed on the computer's screen. Images are made up of many thousands of these tiny dots that the human eye merges into continuous tones.

PPI

Pixels Per Inch. Screen resolution is defined in terms of pixels per inch. It is the number of pixels that a digital image contains in an inch. The higher the PPI, the more detail in the image, but the larger the file size.

Resolution

The amount of detail in a digital image. A high-resolution image has more pixels in it than a low-resolution image. Resolution is commonly given in terms of pixels per inch. For example, a high-resolution 300ppi image would be used for print, while a low-resolution 72ppi image would be used for the Web. Images with a higher resolution need to be larger files to contain the extra data.

RGB

Red, Green, Blue. The most common image mode for digital images. Computer monitors display all colors by mixing the RGB primaries. Other modes include Grayscale for black-and-white-images and CMYK (Cyan, Magenta, Yellow, Black) for professional printed images.

USB

Universal Serial Bus. USB is a format used for connecting many types of device to a computer. The name is used to describe both the socket and the cable. Old computers used USB 1.1, but modern computers now come with the speedier USB 2.0 format. These are interchangeable, so USB 1.1 devices will work with USB 2.0 sockets and vice versa, but they will only work at the speed of the slowest component.

VIDEO GLOSSARY

AV

Audio-visual. AV is used to denote a device or format that carries both audio and video information. For example, an AV-out plug could carry audio and video information from a camera to a TV.

Camcorder

Camera & Recorder. Originally, video recording devices were split into two units—a camera and a recorder. Camcorders combined both of these into one unit, making the device much more compact, and more portable.

DVD

Digital Video Disc, or Digital Versatile Disc. DVD is a disc-based format for storing digital data. The most common usage is for commercial movie sales. Writable DVDs are also commonly used for storing data from computers, including home videos. There are two competing standards of DVD, DVD+ and DVD-. Most modern DVD drives will write both types of disc, but if you have an old drive you will need to check which type of disc it can burn to before purchasing any blank media.

DV

Digital Video. DV is a video cassette format used in many digital video cameras. It has now been largely superseded by MiniDV—a similar format in a smaller cassette, allowing more compact recording devices.

FPS

Frames Per Second. The standard term for the speed of video. Film is usually displayed at a rate of 24fps, which is considered adequate for flicker-free viewing.

MPEG2

A video compression standard define by the Motion Pictures Experts Group. MPEG2 is the standard format used for both digital broadcast and DVD video distribution.

NTSC

The National Television System Committee standard for video broadcast systems in the U.S.A. NTSC video is encoded into 525 screen lines at 29.97fps with a refresh rate of 60Hz.

PAL

Phase-Alternating Line. PAL is a television broadcast standard used throughout Europe and much of the world. The PAL system encodes video into 625 screen lines at 25fps with a refresh rate of 50Hz.

SCART

Syndicat des Constructeurs d'Appareils Radiorécepteurs et Téléviseurs. A single-plug standard for connecting AV devices, for example, a VCR to a television. The standard is common throughout Europe, but in much of the rest of the world, separate RCA connections are used.

Super8

Super8 film was first introduced by Kodak in 1965 as a simple means of creating home movies. The film came in a canister for ease of loading, and ran to 2½ minutes at 24fps. The film could also be run at 18fps to extend the recording time to 3 minutes 20 seconds. It was a hugely popular format, and was only discontinued by Kodak in 1997.

S-Video

Separate Video. S-Video is a connection standard for carrying video data. The video signal is separated into brightness and color components allowing for better quality than traditional composite video that is carried as one component.

Telecine

The name of the process—and the machine used in the process—of transferring old analog video film into digital. The machine essentially works like a digital camera, but instead of light coming through the lens onto a CCD, it is instead shone through the film stock onto the CCD. More expensive devices may split the white light into red, green, and blue components before sending it to three separate CCDs to be recorded.

VHS

Video Home System. The most common recordable format for home videos. Although DVDs are now replacing VHS casettes for commercial movie playback, VHS is still more commonly used for home recording and playback.

MUSIC GLOSSARY

Bit rate

A "bit" is the smallest unit of digital data. The bit rate is the transfer speed of bits, and therefore data, over a unit of time, usually seconds. This is often seen written in megabits per second (Mbps), meaning 1,000,000 bits per second.

Breakout box

Many professional-level sound cards come with breakout boxes. Essentially, these contain miscellaneous connection sockets that would not fit on the faceplate of the sound card itself.

Decibel

A decibel (dB) is (in audio terms) a logarithmic measure of the ratio between sound intensity and sound power. Essentially, it describes the sound level relative to a reference 0 amount. In some cases this can describe the loudness of a sound, in others it can describe the difference in loudness.

Flash memory

A digital storage format. Essentially, it is a chip that can be written to multiple times, but keeps the data stored on it even without power; unlike computer memory (RAM) that loses its content when the power is turned off.

Hz

Hertz. A unit of frequency, meaning per second. If something had a frequency of 1Hz, it would happen once every second. In audio recordings, this is most commonly encountered as kilohertz (kHz), meaning 1,000 times per second.

Line In/Out

Line In is the term used to describe the line level input socket on a speaker system or computer sound card. Line Out is the opposite: the line level output socket on the playback device.

Line Level

Line Level audio refers to a signal that has been passed through a preamp to bring it up to level ready to be amplified by speakers or headphones. Many personal audio devices, such as MP3 players have a Line Out setting that must be activated before playing the device through external speakers.

LP

Long Play. LP is the common term for a vinyl record. More specifically, it refers to the 12" discs rather than the smaller, 7" EPs (Extended Play) commonly used for singles.

MiniDisc

An audio storage format developed by Sony. MiniDiscs store digital data on a small disc held in a plastic case. Although smaller and less liable to scratching than CDs, the format never really caught on, and has now been superseded by MP3 players.

Noise

Noise refers to sounds intruding onto a recording. Normally this will be in the form of tape hiss, or electrical hum caused by poorly insulated components or cables.

Phono

Short for Phonograph. A device for playing back vinyl records, also known as a turntable or record player.

Preamp

The preamplifier amplifies a low-level signal to line level so that it is suitable for passing to a power amp in a speaker system. All phono signals need to pass through a preamp. The amp is often built into the turntable, but it can be a separate box.

RCA connection

Named after the Radio Corporation of America, who introduced this type of connection for linking phono machines to radios. Most audio systems contain these connections, usually in the form of red- and white-colored stereo plugs.

RIAA

The Recording Industry Association of America. A trade body that standardized vinyl record production in America, including the playback "curve" required to achieve the correct sound from a record, known as the RIAA Curve.

Ripping

A common name for the process of transferring digital music data from a CD to a computer.

DOCUMENTS GLOSSARY

File Extension

The three-letter suffix appended to all files on a PC, and many files on modern Macs. It tells the computer which application should be used for opening the file, e.g. DOC denotes a Word document.

Floppy Disk

A disk of plastic that data can be written onto for transfer between computers. It was so named to differentiate it from the metal platters of "hard disks." Originally, the term was used for 5¼" disks that were stored in a flexible plastic case, but 3½" disks, which were in hard plastic cases, were also called floppy disks.

OCR

Optical Character Recognition. Many scanners come with basic OCR software, but these may not work as well as professional packages. Essentially, when a document containing text is scanned into the computer, the OCR software analyzes the image and turns the text in the image into an editable text document.

PDF

Portable Document Format. A file format created by Adobe for storing documents made up of text and images. The files can be viewed in the freely downloadable Acrobat Reader software.

Scanner

A device for transferring artwork or documents to a computer. Most home scanners are of the "flatbed" variety, meaning that they have a glass "bed" that the document is placed on. The scanner head then passes underneath the glass, capturing an image of the document.

Zip Disk

A mostly obsolete disk format. Zip Disks were introduced by Iomega in 1994 as a high capacity (100MB) format for transferring data between computers. They were especially popular with the graphics and design industries where files were often too big to fit on standard floppy disks. They have now been superseded by CDs.

COMMUNICATION GLOSSARY

HTML

HyperText MarkUp Language. The language that underpins the vast majority of websites. Many Web-design programs will handle all of the HTML coding for you, but it's worth familiarizing yourself with a few of the more common commands if you have your own website.

IMAP

Internet Message Access Protocol. A method of retrieving e-mail from a server. In contrast to the more common POP method, IMAP normally leaves the messages on the server, allowing the mail box to be accessed from multiple accounts.

.Mac

An online service offered by Apple, where users can access a number of services for a monthly subscription fee. Services include Web hosting, off-site data storage, e-mail accounts, address book synchronization, among other things.

POP

Post Office Protocol. A method of retrieving e-mail from a server. POP3 is the most up-to-date version, and is used by many e-mail clients. POP covers the retrieval of new mail from a server, and usually the deletion of the mail from the server once it's on the user's machine.

RSS

Really Simple Syndication. A method of keeping track of updates to websites or blogs without having to visit them every time. RSS "feeds" contain basic information—usually a brief description of the update—that is collected by an RSS reader. Users subscribe to any feeds of sites that interest them.

VoIP

Voice over IP (Internet Protocol). The method by which voice communication can be sent over the Internet, or similar network. Used for making phone calls over the Net.

index

acknowledgments

Colin Barrett (Video) would like to thank:
"The PR staff working on behalf of Pinnacle Systems, Sony UK,
Apple Computer UK, Ulead Systems, Canopus and Miglia UK
for their invaluable help with hardware and software. I would also
like to thank my wife Sylvia and family for unknowingly contributing
their services as photographic models, yet again. Finally, a big
thank you to all the regulars on the SimplyDV Bulletin Board
forums for their inspiring ideas and continued support."

Steve Luck (Photographs) would like to thank:
"All the family and friends who generously allowed precious family
photographs to be used in the creation of this title."

Keith Martin (Documents & Communication) would like to thank:
"Everyone who's ever asked me to explain myself more clearly.
You keep me on my toes."

Allen Zuk (Music) would like to thank:
'My friends and fellow DIY musicians Staff Glover and Adam Flood
for their encouragement, support, and helpful comments."